HOPE

BEYOND TOMORROW

MARK A. FINLEY

REVIEW AND HERALD® PUBLISHING ASSOCIATION

Since 1861 | www.reviewandherald.com

A Personal Message From Mark Finley

During the past 50 years I have traveled the world sharing the truths of God's Word with millions of people. Recently I have noticed that more and more people are concerned about the future. "Concerned" may not be a strong enough word. Many of them are afraid. They are afraid of the world their children will be brought up in, or even afraid that the world as we know it now might not exist then. This book is not about fear. It is about hope.

I am convinced that you did not pick up this book because you wanted to be frightened with all the grim statistics of evil in our world. You hold this book in your hands because you want hope—hope for today, tomorrow, and forever. Every chapter of this book is filled with a message of hope. In these pages you will discover a God who loves you more than you can ever realize, and this God has an incredible plan for your life. You will read about God's rescue plan for this wayward planet and understand more completely the events that are even now unfolding in our world. But best of all, you will have divine insight from the Word of God how this world will end. The end of sickness, sorrow, tears, and death is coming soon, for Jesus promises us a whole new world. Soon He is coming to take you home, and that's what this book is all about, so read on and be filled with hope.

Mark Finley

———⊤———

Chapter 1

To Hope Again

In 1991, when the former Soviet Union was falling apart, I gave a series of Bible lectures in Moscow's famed Kremlin auditorium. Thousands of Russians seeking meaning in their lives attended our prophetic series each evening. Bible truths came alive. New hope dawned in their hearts. New peace filled their souls. It was amazing to me to see how these honest-hearted Russians so steeped in atheistic Communism had a longing deep within for something better.

Our meetings were featured in the Russian media daily. As a result, I received an invitation to speak to a group of Russian scientists in a city of about 25,000, one of the Soviet Union's closed cites. Even Russian citizens were unable to enter the city without a special permit. In the 1950s, during the time of Nikita Khrushchev, this city became a center for experimentation in biological and chemical warfare. Hundreds of Russian scientists were settled here from throughout the Soviet Union. Here many of the scientific geniuses of the nation settled and worked in laboratories conducting sophisticated biological experiments.

I was invited to speak for three consecutive nights to these scientists and their families. My topics were "Is the Bible Reliable?" "Who Was Jesus and Was He Really the Divine Son of God, or Was He Just a Moral, Ethical Teacher?" And last: "Is There Any Hope for the Future?" When I arrived at the cultural center for my lecture, I was amazed that the auditorium was packed. More than 1,000 scientists and their families crowded into the lecture hall. The first two nights went extremely well. The Soviet scientists listened intently, asked intelligent questions, and responded favorably. It was the final meeting that gripped their attention most. They wanted to know, in a nuclear world where human beings have the capacity to destroy most of life on Planet Earth, is there hope? They wondered how we could face the future with confidence. Could we march into the future with the assurance that a new world is coming, or are we headed for doomsday?

Hope on the Horizon

The one thing these Russian scientists wanted more than anything else was hope, and the Bible is full of hope. The apostle Paul especially is the apostle of hope. Writing to the Roman church, he encourages the members with these words: "For whatever things were written before were written for our learning, that we through patience and comfort of the Scriptures might have hope" (Romans 15:4). The fifteenth chapter of Romans concludes with these words: "Now may the God of hope fill you with all joy and peace in believing, that you may abound in hope by the power of the Holy Spirit" (verse 13). In troublous times God's Word fills our hearts with hope. In life's trying experiences God's Word fills our hearts with hope. When the future seems uncertain, God's Word fills our hearts with hope.

There is hope on the horizon. Writing to his young

companion Titus, the apostle Paul assures him to keep "looking for the blessed hope and glorious appearing of our great God and Savior Jesus Christ" (Titus 2:13). All of history is moving to one grand climax in the coming of our Lord Jesus Christ. History had a beginning point, and history will have an ending point. All of history began when God created this world, and the climax of Creation is the return of our Lord, who will eventually re-create a new heavens and new earth.

There are three great events in the Bible—Creation, the cross, and the coming of Christ. The return of our Lord to this desperate planet longing for hope is the climax of the ages. It begins the culmination of the long drama of sin and death. The Old Testament prophets and the New Testament disciples heralded it. The angels affirmed it, and Jesus promised it.

The psalmist David triumphantly declared, "Our God shall come, and shall not keep silent: a fire shall devour before Him, and it shall be very tempestuous all around Him" (Psalm 50:3). Paul echoed it as he proclaimed, "The Lord himself shall descend from heaven with a shout, with the voice of the archangel, and with the trump of God: and the dead in Christ shall rise first" (1 Thessalonians 4:16, KJV). Even the angels at Christ's ascension affirmed it. As the disciples strained their necks and squinted their eyes at our ascending Lord, looking longingly into heaven, two angels standing by said, "Men of Galilee, why do you stand gazing up into heaven? This same Jesus, who was taken up from you into heaven, will so come in like manner as you saw Him go into heaven" (Acts 1:11). Jesus Himself promised He would return when He clearly stated to His disciples, "I will come again" (John 14:3). The second coming of Christ is the ultimate answer to the great questions of life—those issues that we struggle with that seem to defy solutions.

The Second Coming of Christ and Life's Great Questions

The second coming of Christ is the solution to the problem of loneliness, low self-esteem, despair, hopelessness, and that nagging emptiness within our hearts. Deep within every human being is the desire to love and be loved. We were made to experience unconditional love based not on what we do but on who we are. There is that innate desire for companionship. We were not made to be alone.

Scientists studying rats noticed that mother rats often licked their young. At first they thought that this might be some sort of bathing. The more they studied the phenomenon, however, the more they concluded that the mother rat was not bathing her babies. Rather, she was love-licking them. The licking was a form of embracing. Further research revealed that when the baby rats are separated from their mothers at a very young age but still provided with the essentials of life, they die at a younger age. Evidently the licking provides a sense of security . . . a sense of belonging . . . a sense of identity.

We all need this sense that someone cares. Every one of us has this longing to be loved unconditionally. To be accepted as we are, no matter where we are from or what we have done in the past. Revelation 21:3 affirms that one day when Jesus returns we will be with God forever. The apostle John joyfully exclaims, "Behold, the tabernacle of God is with men, and

He will dwell with them, and they shall be His people. God Himself will be with them and be their God." The tabernacle of God is the very dwelling place of God. John promises that one day soon we will live with Him forever.

We were not made to live apart from Him. We were made for Him. He will fill the emptiness of our lives. As Augustine said so well centuries ago: "Lord, we were made for You, and our hearts will never find rest until they find rest in You." The ultimate answer to the problem of this cosmic loneliness, this angst within our souls, is the coming of Christ, when we will be in the presence of God forever.

The One who knows us best loves us most and is soon coming to take us home with Him. We can look forward to a future that is bright with the promises of God—a forever future with Him. We are not specks of cosmic dust in the universe. We were created for fellowship with the God that made us. We have a place to belong. One day we will see Him face to face and be immersed in His love. He has promised never to forsake us. Daily He longs to be our companion. The friendship we enjoy with Him today is just a slight foretaste of the deeper fellowship and greater joy we will experience with Him throughout all eternity. Although today we cannot see Him and communicate with Him face to face, the promise of His return reassures us that one day we will see Him and live with Him eternally.

One day we will live in His presence. One day love will reign supreme, and our hearts will be at peace. One day the longing inside to be fully loved with no barriers between will be gone.

The second coming of Christ is not only the answer to

loneliness. It is also the ultimate solution to the problem of pain.

Solving the Problem of Pain

Pain, suffering, sorrow, and tears plague our world. Heart disease, stroke, cancer, and diabetes afflict hundreds of thousands of people each year. In cancer wards across the country patients have had their bodies weakened through multiple surgeries, chemotherapy, and radiation therapy. They have lost their hair, their strength, their energy—and some have even lost their will to live. Disease of all kinds ravages our bodies.

In many of the developing countries malaria is still a major problem. Dysentery and diarrhea, which are often a result of a polluted water supply, cause immeasurable suffering to the very young and old alike.

Natural disasters appear suddenly, seemingly out of nowhere, to destroy homes and leave a wake of suffering and sorrow in their path. Uncontrollable forest fires fueled by fierce winds sweep down canyons and destroy entire communities. The ravages of war cause untold misery. Bombs drop. Battling forces rampage villages, towns, and cities. Children are maimed. Legs are blown off by indiscriminate blasts on innocent civilians. Often in the horrors of war, the women and children suffer the most.

When our bodies are racked with pain because of some dreaded disease, when our lives are turned upside down because of some natural disaster, and when the ravages of war invade our land, we can still find true comfort in the fact that one day Jesus will return, and all our pain and sorrow will be over.

When your body is racked with pain so intense that you cannot think, when you are overwhelmed with grief, anger, and fear and are asking, "Why me, Lord?" remember that suffering will not last forever. Pain will not last forever. Tears and sorrow will not last forever. Jesus is coming again.

Isolated from his family and friends, suffering alone on the isle of Patmos, as a prisoner for the Lord, the apostle John wrote these encouraging words: "And God shall wipe away all tears from their eyes; and there shall be no more death, neither sorrow, nor crying, neither shall there be any more pain: for the former things are passed away" (Revelation 21:4, KJV).

With all our advances in medical science as marvelous as they are, we have not discovered the answer to the problem of pain and suffering. The sophisticated technology of our time has not found a solution to sickness. We have made some giant advances in treating various diseases, but our generation still gets sick. We still suffer. We still experience pain.

I think of my own father, who died several years ago. He suffered with heart disease. His body was afflicted with diabetes. As he aged, his weakened body experienced remarkable pain, but he never complained. He believed that a better day was coming. His hope was anchored in the return of our Lord. He fixed his mind on the day that Jesus would burst through the clouds to take him home. One day when we were talking, he made—in his frail condition, suffering from multiple afflictions—a comment that I will never forget. He said, "Son, I am not afraid to die, because when I do, the next thing I will know will be Jesus coming in the sky to take me home."

He looked beyond his suffering. He saw beyond his pain.

His mind was fixed upon eternity. For Dad, the second coming of Christ was a reality he grasped by faith. He lived in the light of Christ's return. The second coming of Christ is the ultimate answer to the problem of human suffering. It's the only answer to this world's agonizing pain. The epidemic of human suffering and the rivers of human tears cry out for it all to end.

When you suffer, when your body is racked with pain, when you can't stand it another day, when your eyes are filled with tears, you can hope again. You can look away from your suffering because you know that regardless of what happens to you, there is a God that loves you with an everlasting love. He will put an end to all disease, suffering, sorrow, pain, and tears. One day all the trials of this life will be over. One day war will be no more. One day there will be no more natural disasters. One day we will live in a land in which sickness is gone forever, and we will experience life to the full. In that new world joy will abound, and our bodies will pulsate with the vibrancy of health.

The Answer to the Problem of Injustice

Often life seems very unfair. When people sometimes say that we get what we deserve in life and that life is fair, they often have never experienced what some people go through. There are times that we do suffer because of our own poor choices, but there are millions of people who suffer through no choice of their own.

When a baby is born to a crack cocaine addict and suffers from a horrible addiction at an early age, or a child is born HIV positive because of the poor choices of a mother, that is unfair. The child did not make that choice. Think of the Christian teenager driving home from school who is hit by a drunk driver and killed, while the drunk walks away from the accident unharmed. Consider the children whose village is bombed out and who suffer immeasurably or the poverty-stricken country devastated by drought and famine. Imagine the children who are starving to death around the world. In so many instances it was not the individual's choice at all, but circumstances that brought about untold suffering.

Where is fairness when your husband leaves you for another woman? You have raised your children together. Now they are married and out of the home, and you are alone. Where is fairness when you have lived a decent life and you get cancer, but your smoking, alcohol-abusing neighbor with the unhealthy diet seems to do well?

Life may not be fair, but God is always fair. When life kicks us in the stomach and knocks our breath out, He is there to encourage, support, and strengthen us. He is there to remind us constantly that He is coming again to make all things new.

The Bible's last book, Revelation, provides the answer to the problem of injustice. In Revelation 21:5 our Lord says, "I make all things new." One day the King of righteousness will reign. Christ will sit upon His heavenly throne. He will make all things new. Throughout all eternity justice will prevail. We may not be treated fairly here, but we will be then. Justice may not always take place on earth, but in heaven God will make all things right. Justice may not always be meted out by human beings, but it has been established by God as an eternal principle of His government. When you have been treated unfairly, look beyond the injustice to the kingdom of God, when all things will be set right. When you have been cruelly treated, look beyond the hurt to God's new society, where Jesus will reign in righteousness.

Her Affliction Made Her Better, Not Bitter

When Joan Herman was 17 years old, she radiated with the idealism of youth. She spent the summer of 1948 working in a Quaker work camp as a volunteer in the hills of Pennsylvania. Her great desire was to help these impoverished mountain people improve the quality of their lives. Along with other volunteers she spent hours each day digging irrigation ditches to bring running water to some of the remote areas.

It was in the summer of 1948 that a polio epidemic spread through the midwestern and eastern United States. Joanie's symptoms started simply at first. They began with what appeared to be a severe cold, then progressed to an extremely high fever combined with chills and profuse sweating. The muscle pain became intense. She was absolutely fatigued. She could hardly stand it. The back pain became unbearable. She often leaned over her shovel and pushed against the warm earth in the ditch she was digging. Rubbing her back against the drainage ditch wall seemed to give her some modest relief from the intense pain.

One day while trying to continue her work, she was seized with pain that was so bad she collapsed in the ditch. Now it was impossible for her to continue. After a series of medical tests, the diagnosis was polio. As her disease progressed she was paralyzed from her neck down. There was nothing medical science could do to cure her from the dreaded disease.

Her medical providers arranged for her to be placed in a

large pressurized cylinder with only her head sticking out. Since her lungs were also affected by polio, her so-called iron lung was the only way to maintain her breathing.

Joanie survived in this iron lung for 20 years and became the longest living survivor in an iron lung in history. My wife and I met her when we were in our early 20s. She was a remarkable woman with an amazingly optimistic attitude. She helped found a comprehensive community for individuals like her—individuals with severe physical disabilities. Her affliction led her to search for deeper meaning in life. This quest led eventually to serious Bible study and reflection upon God's Word. Day by day she immersed her mind in the hopeful message of the Scriptures. Although she was completely paralyzed, she managed to read the Bible that was mounted on a stand attached to her iron lung. The hope of the coming of Christ inspired her that one day she would be whole again. Passages like these brought her enormous joy.

"The eyes of the blind shall be opened, and the ears of the deaf shall be unstopped. Then the lame shall leap like a deer, and the tongue of the dumb shall sing" (Isaiah 35:5, 6).

"And the inhabitant will not say, I am sick" (Isaiah 33:24).

"Behold, I make all things new" (Revelation 21:5).

Joanie was able to look beyond her pain. She was able, with eyes divinely anointed, to grasp the reality that Jesus was coming again. Polio did not conquer her. She conquered it. Her buoyant, positive spirit touched the lives of countless others. She used her iron lung as a pulpit to proclaim God's love to all who entered her room. They came to minister to her, but she ministered to them. Person after person accepted Christ and the message of Scripture because of her witness. What enabled her to hang on despite life's unfairness? By faith she believed that a better day was coming. The hope of the coming of Jesus burned brightly in her heart. She looked beyond the confines of her iron lung to the day that she would leap and run through fields of waving grain beside the crystal-clear waters of eternity. She had the assurance that Jesus would make all things right, and to the degree that she suffered she would rejoice. She trusted the God who would come to take her to her eternal home.

Cancer is unfair, but one day it will be done away with. War is unfair, but one day it will end. Poverty is unfair, but one day there will be prosperity for all. Famine is unfair, but one day there will be abundance. We can hope again because this earth is not the end of the road, and God will ultimately set all things right.

Death, the Final Enemy, Will Be Defeated

The second coming of Christ is the only answer to the problems of aging and death. No wrinkle-free cream will keep you from aging. No cosmetic surgery will keep the years from marching by. No eye bag job or eyelid operation will keep you looking young forever. There is no magic potion or formula. Hair transplants to combat baldness won't do it.

Although a healthy diet and adequate exercise may extend your life for a few years, they are not the secret of eternal life. Everyone who is born will one day die, unless Jesus returns first. Throughout history people have faced death in a variety of ways. Some have faced it with fear and absolute horror. Others have faced it with hopeless despair, but there are those who have faced death with the absolute confidence and assurance that death is a rest until the glorious resurrection morning, when Jesus shall return. They have faced death with the hope of Christ's return radiating in their hearts.

There is a glorious reunion day coming. When a child dies young, it is not goodbye forever, but goodbye until the morning. When a teenager is killed in an auto collision, it is not goodbye forever, but goodbye until the morning. When a middle-aged man dies from a heart attack, it is not goodbye forever, but goodbye until the morning.

The apostle Paul echoes these marvelous words, "Behold, I tell you a mystery: We shall not all sleep, but we shall all be changed—in a moment, in the twinkling of an eye, at the last trumpet. For the trumpet will sound, and the dead will be raised incorruptible, and we shall be changed. . . . Then shall be brought to pass the saying that is written, 'Death is swallowed up in victory' " (1 Corinthians 15:51–54).

Have you lost a loved one by death? Have you laid a child to rest on some grassy hillside? Has your wife, your husband, your son or daughter, been stricken with some fatal disease? Does the grief seem too much to bear alone? Jesus will carry you through. Listen to His voice encouraging your heart. There is a better day coming. You can hope again. The second coming of Christ is the answer to aging. It is the answer to death, to tears, and to sorrow. In loneliness you can hope again. In discouragement you can hope again. In pain you can hope again. In disappointment you can hope again. In injustice you can hope again. In tears you can hope again. Jesus is coming, and that is the best news anyone can possibly imagine.

Chapter 2

Three Secrets of Lasting Peace

In a recent survey of Americans, participants were given a list of items and asked which they considered a daily necessity. In other words: "What do you need to get through your day? What can't you live without?"

Are you ready for America's priority?

Here is a breakdown of what Americans consider most essential.

37 percent said coffee.

28 percent said sweets.

19 percent said social media.

16 percent said the Bible.

More than twice as many people said their need for coffee was greater than their need for the Word of God.

Could the neglect of God's Word by the average American be one of the significant reasons that so many lack lasting peace, inner contentment, and permanent joy?

Could it be that thousands are looking for peace where peace cannot be found?

Could it be that they are looking in all the wrong places to calm their troubled spirits?

Could it be that there is something better than a cup of coffee to get us through the day?

Hopelessness Leads to Despair

Worry, anxiety, fear, and hopelessness have led millions to experience major depression, which affects about 20 percent of the world's population at some point in their lives. The World Health Organization predicts that by 2020, depression will rival heart disease as the health disorder with the highest disease burden in the world.

Worldwide sales of antidepressants are now approximately $12 billion. There are more than 270 million prescriptions of antidepressants sold in the United States alone each year, but few people consider the downside. One study found that 14 percent of the young people taking an antidepressant became aggressive and even violent.

According to statistics on alcohol abuse and alcoholism by the World Health Organization, about 140 million people throughout the world suffer from alcohol-related disorders, and on average, one person dies by suicide every 40 seconds somewhere in the world. Global suicide rates have increased 60 percent in the past 45 years. There is something tragically wrong when millions of people have lost hope.

The general angst in our society, this inner sense that something is not right and that there is little that is certain, this fear about the future, has created a sense of hopelessness. Hopelessness has contributed to the rise in drug abuse, overmedication with antidepressants, alcoholism and suicide. Thousands of people feel as if they are trapped in a time machine catapulting toward the future and that there is little they can do about it. Someone shouts, "Stop the world. I want to get off."

Hope Makes a Difference

When we lose hope, dark clouds of despair hang over our heads. The future appears gloomy and everything about tomorrow uncertain. But hope leads us from what is to what can be. It paints tomorrow in an array of bright colors. It lifts our spirits from the mud below to the heavens above.

Ana Jacob put it beautifully when she wrote, "The wings of hope carry us, soaring high above the driving winds of life."

William Shakespeare added, "The miserable have no other medicine but only hope."

Hope is not some wishy-washy, vague longing for a better future. It is not baseless desire or an uncertain expectation with no real certainty or assurance. In the ancient Scriptures hope is a strong, confident expectation based on the unchangeable promises of God with the certainty that the thing you hope for will be accomplished.

In His final major discourse to His disciples, Jesus gives them three reasons to be filled with hope. He shares three eternal principles of inner peace. If you really grasp these principles and put them into practice in your life, you will never be the same again. You will experience a new sense of peace. Your life will be filled with hope, and you will live in the joy of our Lord daily.

Jesus' Three Secrets of Lasting Peace

We find these principles in John 14. Before leaving His disciples, Jesus gave them three life-changing assurances.

Secret 1: Never lose hope that Jesus will return. His promise is sure.

He begins His words of encouragement to His disciples by saying, "Let not your heart be troubled; you believe in God, believe also in Me. In My Father's house are many mansions. . . . I go to prepare a place for you. And if I go to prepare a place for you, I will come again and receive you to Myself; that where I am, there you may be also" (John 14:1–3).

If I were translating the expression "Let not your heart be troubled" literally, I would translate it this way: "Stop being so distressed. Don't worry!" Why would the disciples be distressed? Why were their hearts filled with such anxiety?

In John 13 Jesus had just announced that one of the disciples would betray Him and that Peter would deny Him. The disciples had been with Jesus for three and a half years, and they discerned that something was tragically wrong. They could tell from the serious look on His face and the tone of His voice that something climactic was soon to happen. Soon He would face the farce of a trial, the injustice of Pilate's courtroom, the agony of a bloody Roman scourging, the loneliness of the cross, and the shame of bearing the guilt of this world's sin.

These disciples had given their lives for Him. Peter, James, and John had left their fishing boats and nets behind. Matthew had walked away from the tax collector's booth. Each of the disciples had sacrificed to follow Him. Now He was going to a place where they could not follow. Now they were going to be alone. Now they would have to face life's trials and adversities without Him. Now they would have to experience the challenges before them without His personal counsel to guide them.

They were confused, perplexed, worried, and troubled. There was an inner angst, a poverty of soul, a restlessness, an absence of inner peace.

Jesus' words come echoing down the centuries. Let not your heart be troubled. Stop worrying. There is no need to be anxious. This world is not all there is. Cling to My promise. Trust My word. "You believe in God, believe also in Me. I go to prepare a place for you. . . . I will come again."

The promise of Christ's soon return lifts our spirits. It encourages our hearts. It brightens our days. It illumines our nights. It makes every mountain we climb easier.

Plenty of Room in My Father's House

Notice a few expressions in this passage. They are a dose of hope for the soul. Jesus says, "In my Father's house are many mansions" (verse 2). The word "mansions" is better translated "abodes," "dwelling places," or "residences." Here is what Jesus is saying: "There is plenty of room in My eternal kingdom. There is no shortage of space. There is room for you."

The Bible's last book makes this point plain. In prophetic vision the apostle John views multitudes redeemed standing before the throne of God in the heavenly courts. He is utterly amazed and joyfully proclaims, "After these things I looked, and behold, a great multitude which no one could number, of all nations, tribes, peoples, and tongues" (Revelation 7:9).

One of the elders asks, "Who are these? Where did they come from?" The response is clear: "These are the ones who come out of the great tribulation, and washed their robes and made them white with the blood of the Lamb. Therefore they are before the throne of God, and serve Him day and night in His temple" (verses 14, 15).

Heaven has enough room for all. The sacrifice of Christ is sufficient for all. The cross of Calvary provides redemption for all who will receive it. Jesus is assuring His disciples that there is plenty of room in heaven for each one of them and that He will come back to take them to Himself. Whatever your past, there is room in heaven for you. You may have denied your Lord, as Peter did, or seriously doubted His Word, as Thomas did, but His love is reaching out to you right now. He has taken your guilt to Calvary's cross. It can be gone forever. Forgiveness can be yours. At the cross we find forgiveness for our past and power for our present. In these verses Jesus is reassuring His disciples that His death would open heaven's door wide for each one of them and that there was plenty of room for them in the Father's kingdom.

Jesus Prepares a Place

What does it mean that Jesus is "preparing a place" for us? It certainly does not mean that He is a construction foreman instructing the angels how to build our heavenly mansions.

Jesus ascends to heaven and in the presence of the Father receives the assurance that His sacrifice is accepted. The gates of heaven are opened for all humanity.

In the blazing light of the great controversy between good and evil in the universe, Jesus assures us that through His grace and because of His death on the cross we can live eternally with Him. He assures us that He will be our advocate, our defense attorney, in heaven's final judgment.

Daniel 7 describes this cosmic judgment. There are ten thousand times ten thousand heavenly beings that gather around God's throne. Heaven's eternal records are open to the universe. With an all-absorbing interest the universe watches. The destinies of the entire human race are now to be settled. Men and women will be eternally saved or eternally lost. Jesus steps forth in the judgment and declares for all those who by faith believe, this man, this woman, this boy, this girl is one of Mine.

Daniel 7:22 triumphantly declares that "judgment was made in favor of the saints of the Most High." We can have lasting peace because the One who died for us lives for us. We can have lasting peace because the One who died for us and lives for us is coming again for us.

Think of the deaths of the disciples. It is commonly believed that each of them suffered a martyr's death except John, but this is what we know for sure.

James was beheaded by Herod.

Peter was crucified upside down, likely in A.D. 66 by Nero's forces.

John was burned in a caldron of boiling oil, then as an old man in his 90s was exiled on the island of Patmos by the emperor Domitian.

The apostle Paul spent years in a damp Roman dungeon and then was likely beheaded about the same time Peter was martyred by Nero in A.D. 66.

Each one of the disciples except John died a martyr's death, yet they were triumphant.

They were faithful in spite of their circumstances. They

were filled with an inner peace that surpassed "all understanding" (Philippians 4:7). They believed Christ's promise. They clung to Christ's Word: "I will come again!" The assurance of the return of our Lord makes the trials of life bearable. The promise of His second coming quiets our hearts, subdues our fears, and relieves our anxieties. No matter what today brings, there is a better world coming tomorrow.

The early Christians discovered the first secret of inner peace. Take the long view. Life on this earth is short and will soon be over. Every challenge you face, every difficulty you experience, every trial you meet, will soon be over. Cling to the promise of Jesus' soon return; let your heart soar with hope, and let peace flood your soul.

Secret 2: Never lose hope. Jesus is available every moment of the day to give us guidance and direction through prayer. He promises to hear our prayers, listen to our petitions, and grant our requests for the glory of His name.

Here is the Word of the Lord in John 14:12–14:

"Most Assuredly, I say to you, he who believes in Me, the works that I do he will do also; and greater works than these he will do, because I go to my Father. And whatever you ask in My Name, that I will do, that the Father may be glorified in the Son. If you ask anything in My name, I will do it."

Jesus' reassurance to His disciples is remarkable. Although He is returning to the Father, He gives them the absolute assurance that they have access to Him every moment of the day through prayer. There is never a moment He is too busy to hear their prayers. He gives us this unwavering promise that "whatever we ask in His name for the glory of the Father" He will do. We can come confidently and ask. When we are troubled, we can ask for peace; when we are anxious, we can ask for His calm; when we are worried, we can ask for His soothing presence.

One of my favorite books is a small volume entitled *Steps to Christ*, which has sold more than 100 million copies. Here is a real gem on finding peace by presenting our deepest longings to the One who cares for us more than we can ever imagine. "Keep your wants, your joys, your sorrows, your cares, and your fears before God. You cannot burden Him; you cannot weary Him. He who numbers the hairs of your head is not indifferent to the wants of His children. 'The Lord is very pitiful, and of tender mercy.' James 5:11, KJV. His heart of love is touched by our sorrows and even by our utterances of them. Take to Him everything that perplexes the mind. Nothing is too great for Him to bear, for He holds up worlds, He rules over all the affairs of the universe. Nothing that in any way concerns our peace is too small for Him to notice. There is no chapter in our experience too dark for Him to read; there is no perplexity too difficult for Him to unravel. No calamity can befall the least of His children, no anxiety harass the soul, no joy cheer, no sincere prayer escape the lips, of which our heavenly Father is un-observant, or in which He takes no immediate interest. 'He healeth the broken in heart, and bindeth up their wounds.' Psalm 147:3, KJV. The relations between God and each soul are as distinct and full as though there were not another soul upon the earth to share His watchcare, not another soul for whom He gave His beloved Son" (Ellen G. White, *Steps to Christ* [Mountain View, Calif.: Pacific Press® Pub. Assn., 1956], p. 100).

When we enter the presence of Christ, we enter into the arena of peace. When we enter the presence of Christ, our hearts are at rest. When we enter the presence of Christ, the Holy Spirit calms our spirits, quiets our thoughts, and soothes our minds.

There is an old song that the Voice of Prophecy quartet used to sing at the end of Pastor H.M.S. Richards' sermons. The hymn was written by a Presbyterian minister by the name of Cleland Boyd McAfee. He is best known for penning the gospel hymn "Near to the Heart of God" after his two nieces died at a very young age of diphtheria.

> "There is a place of quiet rest,
> Near to the heart of God,
> A place where sin cannot molest,
> Near to the heart of God."

Refrain:
> "O Jesus, blest Redeemer,
> Sent from the heart of God,
> Hold us, who wait before Thee,
> Near to the heart of God."

Verse 2:
> "There is a place of comfort sweet,
> Near to the heart of God,
> A place where we our Savior meet,
> Near to the heart of God."

Verse 3:
> "There is a place of full release,
> Near to the heart of God,
> A place where all is joy and peace,
> Near to the heart of God."

As we draw near to the heart of God through the ministry of the Holy Spirit, we long for His soon return. The Holy Spirit places within our hearts an expectancy—a sense that we just cannot wait to see Him face to face. The closer we draw to Christ, the more His coming becomes a reality in our lives. When you love someone—really love them—you long to be with them. When we enter the presence of Christ, our love for Him grows. We cannot wait to see Him coming in the clouds.

The prophet Isaiah puts the very words in our mouths that we shall shout as we see Him coming back, "And it will be said in that day: 'Behold, this is our God; we have waited for Him, and He will save us. This is the Lord; we have waited for Him; we will be glad and rejoice in His salvation' " (Isaiah 25:9).

Here is the third of Jesus' secrets of lasting peace in a chaotic world.

Secret 3: Never lose hope Jesus will never leave us alone. We are not orphans without a Father. He promises that His personal presence through the ministry of the Holy Spirit will be with us always.

Jesus states this eternal truth emphatically. He could not make it plainer. He says, "I will not leave you orphans" (John 14:18).

We are not fatherless. We are not lonely abandoned orphans

on a spinning orb traveling 67,000 miles an hour through the cosmos. One of the worst experiences is to feel alone in the crisis of life.

Jesus assures us that He will send the third person of the Godhead as His personal representative to supply our needs.

John 14:26, 27 puts it this way: "But the Helper, the Holy Spirit, whom the Father will send in My Name, He will teach you all things, and bring to your remembrance all things that I said to you. Peace I leave with you, My peace I give to you; not as the world gives do I give to you."

Jesus is coming again. The promise of His return is certain, but between now and the time of His return He sends us the Holy Spirit, the third person of the Godhead, as His personal representative. The word translated "comforter" in verse 26 (KJV) is the Greek word *parakletos*. This word means comfort, but it is much more than comfort. It is an extremely rich word full of meaning. Literally translated, it comes from two Greek words, *para* and *kleio*.

Para means "alongside of." We get the English word "parallel" from this word. In gymnastics, parallel bars are two bars alongside of each other. The verb *kleio* means to call. The Holy Spirit is the personal presence of Christ called alongside of the believer.

He is a friend who will never leave or forsake us. The Holy Spirit is our:

1. **Encourager**: He lifts our spirits when we are down.
2. **Strengthener**: He strengthens us when we are weak.
3. **Teacher**: He guides us when we are perplexed and do not know the way.

4. **Defender**: He defends us when we are wrongly accused and others misunderstand us.
5. **Comforter**: He applies the healing balm to our soul when we are hurting and sorrowful.
6. **Convicter**: He convicts us when we go astray. He is the still small voice prompting us to duty, convincing us of wrong, and leading us to the right. He reveals the things of God and accomplishes in us a change of heart.
7. **Supporter**: He holds us up when we are about to fall.

A number of years ago while working in Africa helping to build a new school for about 800 needy students and preaching each evening, I was returning from the meetings one evening to my lodge on the Zambezi River at Victoria Falls and in the dark tumbled down a cement staircase. I landed on my knee and immediately felt the pain as it shot up my leg. Because of previous injuries and my fall, I eventually needed knee-replacement surgery. My recovery was a real ordeal. All of my life I have been active. But now, a few days after the surgery, I could manage only a few short steps. One of the things that help me was my walker. It sustained me. It held me up. Without it I was certain to fall.

In a sense we are all broken. We cannot stand on our own. We need someone who supports us, someone to hold us up, someone to keep us from falling. Jesus promised that although He was going away, He would send His Holy Spirit to support us until He returns in glory.

When the renowned preacher G. Campbell Morgan was a young man, he visited two elderly women each week to read the Bible to them. When he read Matthew 28:20, "Lo, I am with you alway, even unto the end of the world" (KJV), he said, "Isn't that a wonderful promise?"

One of the women quickly replied, "Young man, that is not a promise. It is a fact! All of God's promises are facts."

Here are three great facts that will give you lasting peace.

1. Jesus is coming again. There is hope on the horizon. The Prince of Peace will soon descend through the skies to take His children home.

2. Jesus is instantly available to each one of us each moment of the day. He is our refuge, our security, our peace-giver, our shelter in the time of storm.

3. Jesus is ever-present with us through the gift of the Holy Spirit. The Holy Spirit is our friend, our helper, our trusted companion who walks alongside of us to give us lasting peace.

I love that old hymn "Wonderful Peace."

"Far away in the depths of my spirit tonight
Rolls a melody sweeter than psalm;
In celestial strains it unceasingly falls
O'er my soul like an infinite calm.

"Peace! peace! wonderful peace,
Coming down from the Father above;
Sweep over my spirit forever, I pray,
In fathomless billows of love.

"Ah, soul! are you here without comfort and rest,
Marching down the rough pathway of time?
Make Jesus your Friend ere the shadows grow dark;
O accept of this peace so sublime!

"What a treasure I have in this wonderful peace,
Buried deep in my innermost soul,
So secure that no power can mine it away,
While the years of eternity roll!

"I am resting tonight in this wonderful peace,
Resting sweetly in Jesus' control;
For I'm kept from all danger by night and by day,
And His glory is flooding my soul!

"I believe when I rise to that city of peace,
Where the Author of peace I shall see,
That one strain of the song which the ransomed will sing
In that heavenly kingdom will be—

"Peace! peace! wonderful peace . . ."

As you read these pages my prayer for you is that heaven's peace will flood your soul and that your heart will be filled with the hope and joy of His soon return, so read on, my friend.

Chapter 3

Prophecy's Big Picture

The year was 1989. The Berlin Wall fell. Communism crumbled. Like a mighty rushing unstoppable river, change swept across the Soviet bloc countries. Freedom was in the air in Eastern Europe. The Soviet Union opened to the gospel.

Shortly after the fall of the Communist regime, I traveled to the former Soviet Union with a team of pastors to share the Word of God with Soviet citizens who had been denied the privilege of attending public evangelistic meetings for 40 years.

Night after night I preached to packed audiences in the Plekhanov University auditorium in Moscow. In 1991 and 1992 I conducted evangelistic meetings in the prestigious Kremlin auditorium and finally Moscow's Olympic Stadium. One evening after one of our meetings a frail, middle-aged woman approached me and said, "Pastor, I too am a Christian; please come visit me at my home. I would gladly feed you supper." My wife and I graciously accepted her kind invitation.

When we arrived at her very modest apartment, she enthusiastically welcomed us with open arms. We were somewhat embarrassed with all the attention she showered on us. It was obvious she had prepared for two or three days for our visit.

At that time the average monthly salary in Moscow was $28 a month. As I looked at the dinner table laden with fresh fruits and set for a four-course meal I knew she had spent more than her entire month's salary on the meal. My discomfort level grew as this humble family in a little three-room apartment treated us like royalty. They seemed to want to know everything about America. They asked question after question. They wanted to know where we lived, what our house was like, what we liked to eat, and scores of other little details about our personal lives.

To get the attention off us and on her, I simply asked, "What was the most difficult situation you ever faced as a Christian under the Communist regime?" Her lips began to quiver; her body trembled, her hands shook, and she began to sob. My translator gripped my hand and said, "Pastor Mark, back up. Don't lead this poor woman down this pathway of questioning. Her memories are too painful. She may have an anxiety attack." But it was too late.

The locked secrets kept hidden in her heart for decades came rushing out. She responded, "Pastor, the most difficult experience I ever had under Communism was the KGB [Russian secret police] learning that I was teaching my two daughters about Jesus. An informant living in an apartment above me tipped them off. The police discovered I conducted worship with my children each evening. They discovered that we sang Christian hymns and studied the Bible together. I taught them to place all their confidence in Jesus, not the Communist government. One evening the secret police burst into my home and seized my 9-year-old daughter.

"I still remember her sobs. Her cries, 'Mama, Mama, please

help me.' They carried her out the door, and I could do nothing. I was powerless to help her. Pastor, that was 28 years ago, and I have not seen her since." In some of the harshest years of Communism, Christian children who were indoctrinated in the teachings of Christianity and openly shared their Christian views with their friends were under some circumstances taken from their parents and placed in state homes, to be reeducated in the philosophy of the state.

I looked into the tear-stained eyes of that godly woman. I thought of the pain that pierced her heart like a sword. Through her tears her voice broke, and she confidently stated, "Pastor, I know I will see my daughter again when Jesus comes. We will be reunited then. No one will be able to separate us then. We will be together with Jesus forever."

Jesus' Return: Prophecy's Big Picture

This is prophecy's big picture. It is possible to get so caught up in the minute details of prophecy we miss the big picture. The big picture of prophecy gives us hope. Jesus describes it this way.

"Let not your heart be troubled; you believe in God, believe also in Me. In My Father's house are many mansions; if it were not so, I would have told you. I go to prepare a place for you. And if I go and prepare a place for you, I will come again and receive you to Myself; that where I am, there you may be also" (John 14:1–3).

The second coming of Christ provides hope for troubled hearts. Soon Jesus will come. Soon the heartache and sorrows of life will be over. Soon our trials and tribulations will be a thing of the past. Soon suffering and sickness, war and strife, will be no more. Terrorism and the horrible school shootings will cease. Natural disasters with their devastating effects will vanish in the light of Jesus' return.

There may be many things about the future that we wish we knew. There may be many things about prophecy that we wish we could explain. There is something more important than speculating about all the details of prophecy. Some people are fixated about each minute detail of prophecy and think they have all the answers. The most important thing about prophecy is the glorious, incredibly good news that Jesus is coming again.

All prophecies point to Jesus. He is the climax of all prophecy. His return is the focus of all prophecy. History is not an endless cycle of events. All of history is moving toward one colossal event, the second coming of our Lord. Of all 66 books in the Bible, there are two, Daniel in the Old Testament and Revelation in the New Testament, that focus particularly on the climax of history. The ancient Bible prophets bring courage to our generation. Their focus is not on disaster but on deliverance. Their emphasis is not on a coming catastrophe. It is on a coming Christ. They speak not of a tragic ending but of a glorious beginning. Deep within the hearts of people everywhere there is a longing for peace and prosperity, health and happiness, fairness, forgiveness, and forever.

The Prophecies of Daniel and Revelation

In Daniel and Revelation the prophets present a new world; a better world. They help us reach out and touch the kingdom of God. They give us glimpses of eternity. They help us see the big picture.

Let's take a brief journey together through the prophetic books of Daniel and Revelation. Let's catch the inspiration of these hope-filled books. Daniel and John were captives in foreign lands when they wrote their books. In 605 B.C. King Nebuchadnezzar of Babylon attacked and overthrew Jerusalem. Nebuchadnezzar took a significant number of Hebrew youth captive. One of his captives was Daniel.

John was a captive too. The last of the 12 disciples, John was exiled by the Romans on the island of Patmos, off the coast of Greece. Both Daniel and John longed for deliverance. These prophets anticipated the day when sin and suffering would be over—a day when conflict and chaos would be gone. They looked forward to a new tomorrow, when disease, disaster, devastation, destruction, and death would fade away in the glory of a new world. God honored these Bible stalwarts' faithfulness by showing them prophecy's big picture. He opened their eyes to see eternity.

The second chapter of the book of Daniel opens with the dream of the Babylonian king Nebuchadnezzar. "Now in the second year of Nebuchadnezzar's reign, Nebuchadnezzar had dreams; and his spirit was so troubled that his sleep left him" (Daniel 2:1). The king knew that his dream had unusual significance, but he could not remember it. He called the wisest men of his realm together for an explanation. They too could neither recall the king's forgotten dream nor explain its significance. Infuriated, the king threatened them with death. At this crisis moment Daniel stepped forward. He graciously requested time to pray about the unsolved mystery. God intervened. Heaven's mystery was revealed.

The content of the dream is obvious from Daniel's prayer

of thanksgiving. It reveals a God who "changes the times and the seasons; removes kings and raises up kings. . . . He reveals deep and secret things" (verses 21, 22). Since "wisdom and might" (verse 20) are His, God not only knows the future, but is the architect of the future. Bible prophets do not speculate about the future. They do not guess about what might be coming. In the Scriptures they reveal to us what God has revealed to them. Daniel clearly explained what King Nebuchadnezzar had dreamed. "You, O king, were watching; and behold, a great image!" (verse 31). The prophet then described this awesome figure for the king. This huge metallic image had a head of gold, breast and arms of silver, thighs of brass, legs of iron, and feet of iron and clay (verses 31–33). The climax of the king's dream is a massive stone descending from heaven, striking the image on its feet, and finally becoming a mountain that fills the whole earth.

Think of how amazed the ancient king must have been when the prophet Daniel described the minute details of his dream. The king's next question must have been "Daniel, what does all of this mean?" Daniel's explanation of the dream's meaning is just as precise as his description of the dream's content. He begins the explanation with these words: "You are this head of gold. But after you shall arise another kingdom inferior to yours; then another, a third kingdom of bronze, which shall rule over all the earth. And the fourth kingdom shall be as strong as iron" (verses 38–40).

According to God's interpretation through the prophet Daniel, each metal represents a world-dominating empire. The dream depicts the rise and fall of nations. Daniel identifies Nebuchadnezzar's kingdom of Babylon with these words:

"You are this head of gold" (verse 38). The Babylonian Empire ruled the Middle East and extended its dominion throughout the Mediterranean Basin from 605 B.C. to 539 B.C. Gold is a fitting symbol of Babylon. Babylon's chief god, Bel Marduk, was symbolized in a statue of pure gold. This golden image of Bel Marduk sat in a golden-domed temple on a golden throne beneath a golden candlestick before a golden table.

Babylon's lifestyle of luxurious living led Jeremiah the prophet to call Babylon "a golden cup in the Lord's hand" (Jeremiah 51:7). This incredible prophecy in Daniel 2 reveals that Babylon would not rule forever. "Another kingdom" symbolized by the breast and arms of silver would arise.

During a night of drunken debauchery a mysterious hand wrote these words on Babylon's palace wall: "God has numbered your kingdom, and finished it. You have been weighed in the balances, and found wanting. Your kingdom has been divided and given to the Medes and Persians" (Daniel 5:26–28).

There is no guesswork or speculation here. The kingdom that followed Babylon was Media-Persia. Both the Bible and history verify this fact. The famed Cyrus Cylinder housed in the British Museum records the Persian general's attack on Babylon.

The breast and arms of silver (Media-Persia) were overcome by a third empire of bronze. What nation successfully conquered Media-Persia? The Medes and Persians ruled from 539 B.C. to 331 B.C. They were defeated by the Greeks. The brilliant Greek general Alexander the Great led the Greek armies to victory. Daniel 8 describes the Greeks by name as vanquishing the Media-Persians. Both the Scriptures and history agree. The Greeks ruled from 331 B.C. to 168 B.C., when they were defeated by the iron monarchy of Rome.

During the Roman rule of the Caesars, Jesus was born. A Roman governor tried Jesus, and Roman soldiers crucified Him. The Romans ruled from 168 B.C. to approximately A.D. 351. Four metals: gold, silver, bronze, and iron. Four dominant world empires: Babylon, Media-Persia, Greece, and Rome. Did a fifth nation overthrow Rome? Was Rome conquered by another more powerful political power? Certainly not. Rome was overcome by the Germanic barbarian tribes from the north. Listen to these remarkable words from the prophecy: "Whereas you saw the feet and toes, partly of potter's clay and partly of iron, the kingdom shall be divided" (Daniel 2:41).

History has followed prophecy like a builder follows an architect's blueprint. The Roman Empire was divided and remains divided to this day. The prophecy continues with these insightful words: "They will not adhere to one another, just as iron does not mix with clay" (verse 43). Would-be world rulers have tried to revive the Roman Empire.

Each passing century marks the fulfillment of this ancient prophecy. Charlemagne, Charles V, Napoleon, Kaiser Wilhelm, Hitler, Mussolini, and Stalin all attempted to unite Europe through either intermarriage or political conquest. The independent nations of Europe speak eloquently of a God who is in control, a God who guides the destiny of the nations. The prophecy comes to an incredible climax in Daniel 2:44. "And in the days of these kings the God of heaven will set up a kingdom which shall never be destroyed; and the kingdom shall not be left to other people; it shall break in pieces and consume all these kingdoms, and it shall stand forever."

According to this remarkable prophecy the next event on heaven's timetable is Jesus Christ, the Rock of Ages, that Rock cut out without hands, setting up His eternal, everlasting kingdom. The kingdoms of this earth are temporary. God's kingdom will last forever. The reign of earthly kings is short-lived. The reign of Jesus is eternal. The prophecies of both Daniel and Revelation picture one glorious, climatic event on the horizon the return of the Lord Jesus Christ. Each successive prophecy throughout the 12 chapters of Daniel repeats the central theme of the earlier chapters and enlarges upon it. Repetition and enlargement are God's way of helping us understand prophecy's genuine meaning.

Prophecy Repeats and Enlarges
In Daniel 2 God uses the symbol of four metals to describe four mighty kingdoms. In Daniel 7 God uses the symbol of four beasts to describe the same four nations. In Daniel 2 the fourth metal, iron, has 10 toes. In Daniel 7 the fourth beast has 10 horns. The beasts that God chooses to describe these nations are fitting descriptions of each nation. Once again, we do not have to guess at the meaning of this prophetic symbolism. The same God who reveals prophecy explains prophecy. According to Daniel 7:17, "those great beasts, which are four, are four kings which arise out of the earth." A king represents his kingdom. The fact that each beast in Daniel 7 represents a kingdom is made clear in verse 23: "The fourth beast shall be a fourth kingdom on earth, which shall be different from all other kingdoms." In a

magnificent vision God pictured these beasts rising up out of the sea on a fiercely stormy night in the midst of mighty winds.

In Bible prophecy the sea or water represents people (Revelation 17:15). Wind represents destruction, devastation, and disaster (Jeremiah 49:36, 37). Daniel's prophecy predicts nations arising amid the conflict of war and strife.

The first beast, the lion with eagle's wings (Daniel 7:4), is an accurate description of the nation of Babylon. Archaeologists have discovered this "lion with eagle's wings" symbol on the walls of the famed Ishtar Gate of Babylon and on coins excavated from Babylon's ruins.

The Medes and Persians were aptly described in the ruthlessness of a bear with three bloody ribs in its mouth (verse 5). It is interesting to note that for the Medes and Persians to dominate the Middle East they had to conquer three nations—Babylon, Lydia, and Egypt. As the prophecy describes, they devoured three ribs.

The swiftness of Alexander the Great's conquests are graphically revealed in the symbolism of a leopard with wings (verse 6). This third beast, the leopard, has four heads. Why? When Alexander died, his four generals took over his empire. Amid conflict and political intrigue, Cassander, Lysimachus, Ptolemy, and Seleucus divided the territory of the Greek Empire among themselves. The fourth beast is pictured as incredibly fierce and amazingly powerful, with huge iron teeth (verse 7). The image of Daniel 2 has 10 toes. The "dreadful beast" of Daniel 7 has 10 horns (verse 8). Like the 10 toes, the 10 horns symbolize the divisions of the Roman Empire. It is at this point in the prophecy that God introduces a completely new element.

Until now, political powers have attempted to usurp God's rightful position as the one who truly reigns over this earth. In Daniel 7:8 a "little horn" power, a power that begins small but is catapulted into world dominance, grows quietly out of the Roman Empire.

According to the prophecy, this power has "eyes like the eyes of a man" (verse 8). In the Bible, eyes are a symbol of wisdom or understanding (Ephesians 1:18). The authority of this power is human, not divine. It is based on human wisdom, not God's Word. It would ultimately "cast truth down to the ground" (Daniel 8:12).

This new power would "speak pompous words," "persecute the saints of the Most High," and "intend to change times and law" (Daniel 7:25). This little-horn power would be "different" (verse 23) than all other political powers mentioned in this chapter.

Prophecy indicates this power is religious, not political (verse 24, 25). A counterfeit political religious system arises in the Middle Ages attempting to usurp God's authority by changing God's law. God's answer to the challenge of the little horn is His final judgment (verse 21, 22).

God's final judgment establishes our Lord as the rightful ruler of the universe. In the judgment all things are set right. Earthly rulers have attempted to usurp Christ's place, but in the final judgment Christ is established as the rightful ruler of this planet. No political or religious ruler can rival Him.

All the prophecies of Daniel end in the same place—the establishment of God's eternal, everlasting kingdom. Catch the triumphant tone of the final verses of this amazing prophecy.

"But the court shall be seated, and they shall take away his dominion, to consume and destroy it forever. Then the kingdom and dominion, and the greatness of the kingdoms under the whole heaven, shall be given to the people, the saints of the Most High. His kingdom is an everlasting kingdom, and all dominions shall serve and obey Him" (verses 26, 27).

As the earth's kingdoms crumble, God's kingdom lasts forever. The prophecies of Daniel all have one central theme. They have a single sharp focus, the triumph of God's eternal kingdom in the return of our Lord. This is true of all four great lines of prophecy in Daniel 2, 7, 8, and 11. The prophecies of Daniel and Revelation picture the triumph of Christ over all the forces of hell. When He comes again in power and glory and splendor, the kingdoms of this world will become the kingdoms of our Lord. The coming of our Lord is the climax of history. It is the triumph of the kingdom of God over the forces of hell. It is the climax of the great controversy between good and evil.

Revelation's Prophecies, Christ's Triumph

The aged apostle John, a prisoner on the rocky, barren island of Patmos, joyfully writes, "Behold, He is coming with clouds, and every eye will see Him" (Revelation 1:7). Separated from his family, friends, and fellow Christians, John longed to see the One whom his soul loved. John longed for the day when he could sing with the redeemed of all ages, "Blessing and honor and glory and power be to Him who sits on the throne, and to the Lamb, forever and ever!" (Revelation 5:13). This is prophecy's big picture.

The prophecies of Daniel and Revelation focus on much

more than cryptic symbols, bloodthirsty beasts, dreadful dragons, and the antichrist's mark. They speak of a climax of all things. They speak of Jesus and His everlasting kingdom. In Revelation 7 John looks beyond all of earth's coming sorrows to this magnificent scene. "Therefore they are before the throne of God, and serve Him day and night in His temple. And He who sits on the throne will dwell among them" (verse 15).

There is a God-shaped vacuum within us that will never be filled unless God fills it. Our hearts cry out for intimacy with the Creator. We long for God. Since the day Adam and Eve sinned, humanity has felt a sense of loss, an emptiness within. The only thing that can fill this aching void is the reality of God's presence. When Jesus returns, this longing will be fulfilled. The kingdom of God will be restored. The entire universe will sing. There is nothing quiet or silent about this event. This is the coronation of a king! The entire universe shouts it!

Revelation's prophecy of the seven trumpets concludes with these words: "The kingdoms of this world have become the kingdoms of our Lord and of His Christ, and He shall reign forever and ever!" (Revelation 11:15).

Along with Daniel, the prophecies of Revelation graphically describe the destruction of all evil forces at the coming of our Lord. In Revelation 14:19, 20, John pictures God's "sickle" destroying all sin and sinners. In the glorious triumph of the coming of our Lord that is portrayed in Revelation 19, John sees heaven open. Jesus Christ symbolized as a conquering general riding a white horse returns. All evil forces that stand in His way are destroyed. The powers of hell, which battle against His kingdom, are doomed. The "beast" and the "false prophet" are "cast alive into the lake of fire burning with brimstone" (Revelation 19:20). Jesus is exalted as "KING OF KINGS AND LORD OF LORDS" (verse 16).

In Revelation 20 John depicts a desolate earth with Satan bound and the wicked destroyed for 1,000 years (verses 1–3). During this 1,000 years, which some Bible students term "the millennium," the redeemed or saved who have been caught up to meet Christ in the air at His return (John 14:1–3; 1 Thessalonians 4:16, 17) reign with Jesus in heaven (Revelation 20:4). As heaven's books are opened, the saved see clearly that God's love has done everything possible to save every single person.

At the end of these 1,000 years the Holy City descends from heaven to earth. The wicked dead are resurrected. Satan leads these legions of the lost to attack the Holy City (verses 5, 7, 8). The cleansing fire of the presence of God descends from heaven and devours sin and sinners forever. God's holiness purifies the earth.

John describes this almost overwhelming, breathtaking, magnificent scene this way:

"Then I, John, saw the holy city, New Jerusalem, coming down out of heaven from God, prepared as a bride adorned for her husband. And I heard a loud voice from heaven saying, 'Behold, the tabernacle of God is with men, and He will dwell with them, and they shall be His people. And God Himself will be with them and be their God. And God will wipe away every tear from their eyes; there will be no more death, nor sorrow, nor crying. There shall be no more pain, for the former things have passed away' " (verses 1–4).

What a hope! What a destiny! What a bright picture of tomorrow! Beyond our heartaches, sorrow, and tears, Jesus will come. Beyond the disasters of tribulation, Jesus will come as King of kings. He will come as Lord of lords. He will come as the Mighty Conqueror. He will come to reign eternally, and the whole world will know it!

Chapter 4

Facing the Future
With Greater Confidence

In one of his sermons Billy Graham tells a fascinating story about the brilliant scientist Albert Einstein. It seems that Einstein was on a train traveling in Europe when the steward approached him and asked for his ticket. Einstein fumbled through his belongings, searched his pockets, and looked in his billfold, but all his attempts produced absolutely nothing. He just could not find his ticket.

The train's steward simply said, "I know who you are; don't worry about it. I know you have your ticket someplace." And he proceeded up the aisle. When he looked back, he saw Einstein on his knees frantically looking under his seat, desperately searching for his ticket. The renowned scientist seemed awfully distressed that he could not find it.

Attempting to ease his anxiety, the steward said, "Mr. Einstein, I know who you are. Don't worry about it." Einstein replied, "I know who I am too, but I do not know where I am going."

This single sentence reflects the thinking of millions of people in this world. They have little idea of where this world is headed. At best they have some vague, shadowy idea about the future. They are longing for hope beyond tomorrow. The great hope of the return of our Lord gives purpose to our lives today. We can live joy-filled lives filled with hope because we know the end of the story.

Someone has well said, "Life has no value unless you focus on something valuable." There is nothing more valuable than knowing Christ and having the hope of His soon return burning in your heart.

Beyond Despair

I have always been fascinated with the hopeless despair described in the inscriptions on the tombs in the catacombs along the Appian Way just outside of Rome. You will recall that the apostle Paul was led along the Appian Way when he was brought by the Roman authorities as a prisoner to Rome. He must have sensed the despair of the pagan populace of Rome as they lost hope about the future.

Here are just a couple of the inscriptions.

"I was not, I became, I am not, I care not."

"Eat, drink, enjoy yourself, then join me."

In describing life, the skeptic Bertrand Russell put it this way: "We stand on the shore of an ocean, crying out to the night and to emptiness. Sometimes a voice of one drowning, and in a moment the silence returns. The world seems to me quite dreadful, the unhappiness of many people is very great, and I often wonder how they all endure it."

What hopelessness, what despair, what meaninglessness. Again, if you do not have something valuable to live for, something beyond yourself, some hope for tomorrow, some overriding purpose, life has little value.

In the face of scoffing, mocking, and skepticism, the apostle Peter presents the all-consuming purpose of life. He expresses it in these words:

"Beloved, I write to you this second epistle (in both of which I stir up your pure minds by way of reminder), that you may be mindful of the words which were spoken before by the holy prophets, and of the commandment of us, the apostles of the Lord and Savior" (2 Peter 3:1, 2).

There is something of significance here. Some people are always looking for some novel new truth to unlock the mystery of the future. They are trying to discover some revelation that will give them divine insight into what's coming. Millions of people are looking for answers and turning to psychics, Eastern mystics, or New Age gurus. They are always attempting to discover some mystical key to understand this world's destiny. They have this insatiable desire to find the truth about the future.

What Peter says is simply this: what we need is not so much new, novel truth, but a repetition of the eternal truths of Scripture that we so often neglect.

The Bible's Message of Hope

There are certain biblical truths that need to be repeated again and again and never pushed into the background for the sake of novelty. They are eternal revelations of God's plan for this planet's future. The predictions of the biblical prophets have rung true throughout the centuries. We can have confidence in their predictions regarding the future. Although Bible prophecy predicts a coming time of trouble, beyond this trying time God's Word reveals that a bright new world will replace this sin-polluted planet.

The Greeks spoke of "time which wipes things out," as if the mind were a slate and time an eraser. The passage of time often leads us to forget the eternal truths of a past generation. This is precisely why throughout Scripture the great truths are repeated again and again, lest we forget. We do not need something new as much as we need to be reminded of the ancient truths of Scripture that give meaning and purpose to all our lives.

The apostle Peter continues in 2 Peter 3:3, 4. He encourages each one of us to know "that scoffers will come in the last days, . . . saying, Where is the promise of His coming? For since the fathers fell asleep, all things continue as they were from the beginning of creation."

In the last days the idea of the second coming of Christ will appear ridiculous to many people. It will be a subject of ridicule, skepticism, and mockery. They will cynically ask, "Where is the promise of His coming?" Second Peter 3 uses the word "promise" three times. You will find it in verse 4 and in verse 9, "The Lord is not slack concerning His promise," and again in verse 13, "Nevertheless we, according to His promise, look for new heavens and a new earth."

Three times Peter uses word "promise" to describe the certainty of our Lord's return to the scattered believers throughout Asia. God's promises are certain. They have stood the test of time. They are reliable. Jesus put it well in His end-time sermon in Matthew 24. After discussing the signs of His return that include wars and international conflict; famines and natural disasters; rising crime and terrorism; religious oppression on one hand and the gospel speedily going to the ends of the earth on the other, Christ declares, "Heaven and earth will pass away, but My words will by no means pass away" (Matthew 24:35).

The second coming of Christ is not based on idle speculation. It is not based on a vain wish or human philosophy. It is based on the unchangeable, reliable, certain promises of God's Word. The second coming of Christ reveals the tremendous truth that all of history is moving toward one glorious climax, . . . one final destiny—that life is going somewhere, and we are to meet Someone who has the ultimate answer to all of life's problems. And without this conviction there is little left to live for.

A promise is a declaration, an assurance that one will do a thing or that a thing will happen. It is a pledge, a bond, an oath, a contract, a commitment or a covenant. A promise is as good as the one making it, and there can be no greater authority than the Word of God and no greater Promiser than Jesus Himself.

Promises of Christ's Return

Throughout Scripture Christ has promised to return. The promises of Christ's return resound through all of Scripture. Someone has counted 1,500 passages in the Bible that mention Christ's return. The return of our Lord is mentioned once in every 25 verses in the New Testament, and 23 of the 27 books describe it. For every prophecy in the Old Testament regarding the first coming of Christ, there are eight prophecies on the second coming of our Lord. Here are just a few of the Bible passages spanning centuries that reveal that Jesus will return.

One of the earliest prophets to proclaim the glory of the second coming of Jesus was Enoch. Enoch was so close to God that the Bible says that he "walked" with God and eventually was translated to heaven without seeing death. One little boy describing what happened to Enoch put it this way. "Enoch and God used to take long walks together. One day they got closer to God's house than Enoch's house, so God said, 'Enoch, we are closer to My house than your house. Why don't you come home with Me?' " Enoch believed that one day we would all go home with God. Discussing Enoch's prediction, Jude in the New Testament says,

"Enoch, the seventh from Adam, prophesied . . . , saying, 'Behold, the Lord comes with ten thousands of His saints' " (Jude 14).

One thousand years before the first coming of Jesus, the psalmist David predicted not only that Jesus would come once to die for the sins of humanity, but that He would come again to take us home.

David declares, "Our God shall come, and shall not keep silent" (Psalm 50:3).

The prophet Isaiah encourages us with these words:

"Say to those who are fearful-hearted, 'Be strong, do not fear! Behold, your God will come. . . . He will . . . save you' " (Isaiah 35:4).

Zephaniah is one of the many Old Testament prophets whose writings ring with the certainty of our Lord's return.

"The great day of the Lord is near; it is near and hastens quickly" (Zephaniah 1:14).

In one of the most magnificent passages in all of Scripture on the return of our Lord, the apostle Paul states:

"The Lord Himself will descend from heaven with a shout, with the voice of an archangel, and with the trumpet of God. And the dead in Christ will rise first. Then we who are alive and remain will be caught up together with them in the clouds to meet the Lord in the air. And thus we shall always be with the Lord" (1 Thessalonians 4:16, 17).

Standing head and shoulders above all the Bible prophets is Jesus, who promises that He will return.

"Let not your heart be troubled; you believe in God, believe also in Me. In my Father's house are many mansions; if it were not so, I would have told you. I go to prepare a place for you. And if I go and prepare a place for you, I will come again and receive you to Myself; that where I am, there you may be also" (John 14:1–3).

He then adds, "For the Son of Man will come in the glory of His Father with His angels, and then He will reward each according to his works" (Matthew 16:27).

The return of our Lord is not idle speculation; it is reality. It is as certain as the promises of God's Word. Christ has pledged His word that He will return. He longs to come and take us home. He wants you with Him more than you can ever imagine. There is nothing more important to Jesus then our eternal salvation.

Last-Day Scoffers

There are those skeptics who believe that the coming of Jesus is a fairy tale. They see it as a myth or the figment of an overactive imagination. To them it is a vain hope or an idle tale.

What they may not realize is that Bible prophecy describes their condition. Notice what the scoffers say, they skeptically ask, "Where is the promise of His coming? For since the fathers fell asleep, all things continue as they were from the beginning of creation" (2 Peter 3:4).

In other words, there have been no significant changes in the history of the world from the beginning. Things have continued on a uniform basis. Then Peter makes this stunning observation: "This they willfully forget" (verse 5).

One Bible translation puts it this way: "For this they willingly are ignorant of . . ." (KJV). It is one thing to be ignorant but another thing to be "willingly ignorant."

These people had the facts before them, but they scoffed at the facts and denied the truthfulness of God's Word. They were locked in their opinions and would not change. Their minds were made up, and in the face of the clear evidence of revelation they would not change their mind-set or give up their long-cherished habits.

Jesus made this declaration regarding understanding truth, "If anyone wills to do His will, he shall know concerning the doctrine" (John 7:17). Understanding God's will is as much a matter of the heart as it is the mind. God reveals truth to those who are willing to follow truth.

How do you know if you are totally surrendered to God? It is quite easy to sing the song "All to Jesus I Surrender," but what does it mean to surrender all? If there is nothing in my life that I am not willing to give up if He reveals it to me, then I can be certain I am totally surrendered to Him.

Peter now describes three actions of God that prove the scoffers wrong when they emphatically state that "all things continue as they were from the beginning of creation" (2 Peter 3:4).

1. God created the world by His Word in the beginning (verse 5).
2. God destroyed the world at the time of the Flood by His Word (verse 6).
3. God preserves this world each day by His Word (verse 7).

One of the questions that many people ask is: "Why hasn't Jesus come yet? What is delaying His coming?" The apostle Peter proceeds to answer this question and give us one reason for the delay of the return of Christ. God certainly has not forgotten about His promise.

"But, beloved, do not forget this one thing, that with the Lord one day is as a thousand years, and a thousand years as one day. The Lord is not slack concerning His promise, as some count slackness, but is longsuffering toward us, not willing that any should perish but that all should come to repentance" (verse 9).

The apostle makes this key point. God's view of time and ours are dramatically different. For God, time is always eternally present. The past and the future are as vividly real to Him as the present moment is to us. What seems long to us is but a mini-second with God. The heart of a loving God longs for all people to be saved. He waits patiently in mercy for the gospel to be proclaimed to the ends of the earth so that everyone will have the opportunity to respond to His grace, accept His pardon, experience the "new life" He offers, and be ready for His return.

Then he adds this glorious assurance: "But the day of the Lord will come as a thief in the night, in which the heavens will pass away with a great noise, and the elements will melt with fervent heat; both the earth and the works that are in it will be burned up. Therefore, since all these things will be dissolved, what manner of persons ought you to be in holy conduct and godliness . . . ?" (verses 10, 11).

"What sort of person ought you to be?" This is a fascinating expression. It literally means, "What country do you come from?" Here is what Peter is saying: "If you are a Christian, you are a citizen of heaven. You are a pilgrim and stranger on the earth. You are a child of the King. You are an ambassador for Christ, and you ought to act like a citizen of heaven."

Here are three eternal truths of Scripture:

1. God longs for all humanity to be saved. He suffers long. He waits patiently for the gospel to be spread to the ends of the earth (Matthew 24:14). There is nothing that God would not do to save you. The most important thing to God is that you spend eternity with Him. He has given heaven's most precious gift in Jesus to save you. Christ's death on the cross is for you. Christ's forgiveness can be yours. Christ's power can change your life.

2. God waits patiently for us to repent, grow in grace, and reflect His image before a waiting world and a watching universe. He is actively working by His Holy Spirit to accomplish His last-day mission of proclaiming the message of His love to the ends of the earth through

His people. He longs for you to be a witness of His love and grace to the people around you, so they too can be prepared for His soon return.

3. God's justice requires that sin be dealt with soon. It cannot be allowed to continue forever. When evil rises to a certain point, Jesus will say, "It is enough." When the accumulated figures of sin reach a certain amount known only to God, He will say, "Ladies and gentlemen, it is closing time."

When Billy Graham wrote his book *World Aflame,* it is reported that he gave the first chapter to his wife, Ruth, to review. She sat quietly reading this powerful description of world conditions and then looked up and said, "Billy, if Christ does not come soon, He will have to raise Sodom and Gomorrah from the dead and apologize to them, for this generation is certainly more sinful than their generation." The cities of Sodom and Gomorrah passed the point of no return. God destroyed those wicked cities of the plain with a fiery conflagration from heaven.

The civilization in Noah's day also passed the point of no return. They rejected the heaven-sent warnings through Noah, and God destroyed this world with a flood.

The Babylonian Empire under King Belshazzar passed the point of no return. God's finger wrote these words of impending doom on the wall of the palace banquet hall during the night of feasting and revelry: "God has numbered your kingdom, and finished it. . . . You have been weighed in the balances, and found wanting" (Daniel 5:26, 27).

Evil will not have the final word, God will. Wickedness

will not last forever. Sin will not reign eternal. Jesus promises to come again.

As the apostle Peter comes to the end of his second epistle, he gives us this reassuring promise. "Nevertheless we, according to His promise, look for new heavens and a new earth in which righteousness dwells" (2 Peter 3:13).

The entrance requirements for this new society are no less than righteousness, holiness, and sinlessness.

Who is righteous enough to stand before a righteous God?

Who is holy enough to appear before a holy God?

Who alone is without sin to stand before a sinless God?

The apostle Peter shares this eternal truth: "Blessed be the God and Father of our Lord Jesus Christ, who according to His abundant mercy has begotten us again to a living hope through the resurrection of Jesus Christ from the dead, to an inheritance incorruptible and undefiled and that does not fade away, reserved in heaven for you, who are kept by the power of God through faith for salvation to be revealed in the last time" (1 Peter 1:3–5).

We appear before God in Christ. He is our righteousness.

Everything we are not, He is.

All we need is found in Him.

Christ justifies us—in Him we stand before God just as if we had never sinned.

Christ sanctifies us—if we let Him, He will make us what He longs for us to be.

He works in our hearts to change us—to make us over again. In Christ we are accepted as His sons and daughters. As we daily grow in grace, we become more and more like the One we admire.

He is our righteousness. The Sinless One died the death that we deserve so we can live the life He deserves.

In Christ we appear before God just as if we had never sinned.

The One who will one day reign on the throne of the universe longs to reign in our hearts, so we can reign with Him eternally.

He waits patiently in love for each one of us to open our hearts to His transforming grace, to be ready for His soon return.

Ready for His Return

Sir Ernest Shackleton, an Irish-born British explorer, made numerous trips to the Antarctic in the early twentieth century. On one trip disaster struck when his ship, the *Endurance,* was crushed by ice. He and his crew drifted on sheets of ice for months until they reached Elephant Island.

Seeing that his men were on the precipice of disaster, Shackleton led a team of five others out on the water again. They boarded a 22-foot lifeboat and navigated their way toward South Georgia Island. Sixteen days after setting out, the crew reached the island, where Shackleton had to set out on foot, trudging over the snow-covered mountains, blazing trails where there were no trails, in frigid temperatures, to arrive at a small whaling village. He was able to secure a vessel to eventually rescue his crew, all of whom survived the ordeal. Not one of them perished in the icy ordeal. He was gone for months, yet the men left behind never gave up hope.

The icy conditions delayed his return. Three times he tried to reach them, but the seas were so frozen over it was impossible to get to Elephant Island. The sea lanes were clogged with ice. Finally, in his last effort he found a narrow passageway through the ice.

Guiding his small ship back to the island, he was delighted not only to find his men alive but well prepared to get aboard. They were soon on their way to safety and home.

After the excitement of reunion passed, Shackleton inquired how it was that they were ready to get aboard the ship so promptly. Delay could easily have allowed the sea lanes to freeze over and doomed them to death on that uninhabited, barren frigid island. They told him that every morning their leader rolled up his sleeping bag, saying, "Get your things ready, boys; the boss may return today."

During horrible conditions these marooned explorers on an uninhabited island surrounded by ice with little chance of deliverance never gave up hope. They were kept alive by hope. They were inspired by hope. They were motivated by hope. They survived because of hope. Tired, cold, freezing, hungry, isolated, on that frozen speck in the midst of Antarctica they clung to hope. They believed Ernest Shackleton would return, and every day they prepared as if he would return that day.

We too are isolated on this island in space traveling 67,000 miles an hour through the cosmos, filled with terrorism, natural disasters, crime, violence, and immorality, but we have this hope that burns within our hearts. This hope inspires our spirits and encourages our souls. This hope lifts us up and keeps us going day after day in the face of the joys and sorrows of our lives. This hope that deliverance is on the way. This hope that Jesus is coming again. This hope that rescue is near. This hope that one day we will get off this sin-polluted planet in rebellion and head for home with Jesus to live with Him forever.

The only way to be ready for Jesus' soon return is to make an intelligent decision to let Him have complete control of our lives today, tomorrow, and forever.

Chapter 5

Ready for His Return

Have you ever noticed how children are sometimes forgetful? As a lad of 10 or 11 I had difficulty remembering my chores. Mom would often ask,

"Mark, have you made your bed?"
My response: "Oh! Sorry, Mom; I forgot."
"Mark, have you cleaned your room?"
My response: "Oh! Sorry, Mom; I forgot."
"Mark, have you taken out the trash today?"
My response: "Oh! Sorry, Mom; I forgot."

Smiling, she would say, "Mark, if you forget one more time, I will tie a red ribbon around your finger so you will remember."

There are times we forget the things that are important and need a symbolic red ribbon tied around our finger to remember. We need a reminder of the things that are significant. We need someone to help us remember the things that really count in life. It is easy to overlook what matters most. The things of time can crowd out the things of eternity. The problem is not only ours. It existed in the early church, too! New Testament believers were in danger of forgetting the promise of Christ's return.

The Apostle Peter's Reminder

The year was somewhere around A.D. 65. Peter was a prisoner in Rome condemned to death by the Roman emperor Nero. He knew that the end was near. There was one thing on his mind. One dominant picture captured his imagination. One theme filled his thoughts. One truth swallowed up every other:

The Christ he loved, the Christ who redeemed him, the Christ who accepted him despite his failures, gave him the grace to continue in ministry. This Jesus was coming again in power and glory. He had denied his Lord three times at the very moment that Jesus needed him most. But Jesus is the God of the second chance.

Think of the times you have let Him down, the times you have disappointed Him, the times you have broken His heart and He has put His arm around you and whispered ever so gently, "Get up, move on; let's go on this journey together."

Peter writes to believers scattered through Asia in the first century, but his words ring with eternal relevance and come echoing down the corridors of time and speak to our hearts in this time and in this place. He writes to believers living in the real world struggling to keep focused on the things that matter most. The apostle declares: "I will not be negligent to remind you always of these things, though you know and are established in the present truth" (2 Peter 1:12).

The Greek philosophers had a saying that went something like this: "Time wipes out all things."

The passage of time causes us to tend to forget. Peter is concerned about one thing: reminding believers that the second coming of Christ is a reality.

In 2 Peter 1, Peter discusses the certainty of Christ's coming. In 2 Peter 2, the apostle speaks in urgent tones, reminding the first-century believers of the reality of the coming judgment. In the the last chapter of this short epistle, Peter confronts the scoffers head-on to debunk the myth that Jesus may not come at all. He outlines the reasons for the delay of the Advent and makes an urgent appeal for all believers in every generation to be prepared for the return of our Lord.

Peter is speaking not only to his generation but to ours. He is speaking not only to the first-century church but to the twenty-first-century church. He is speaking not only to scattered believers in Asia but to gathered believers everywhere. He writes to remind us of the eternal truth of the return of our Lord.

It is a universal fact that it is easy to get so caught up in the challenges of this life that we forget that one day the journey on this earth will come to an end.

1. **It is so easy to forget**—Life tends to go on as normal. The ebb and flow of life seems to be as it has always been. We are born. We live. The decades pass. We die. I can imagine the apostle Peter shaking his head and saying: "Never forget: death is not the end. There is a divine certainty: Jesus is coming again."

2. **It is so easy to forget**—to become complacent, lackadaisical, halfhearted. Peter says, "Listen to me. There is a divine certainty: Jesus is coming again."

3. **It is so easy to forget**—life presses in on us. There

are family responsibilities, financial pressures, health concerns, and a thousand other distractions, Peter says, "Listen to me. There is a divine certainty: Jesus is coming again."

"The Lord Is Coming, Brother"

Many years ago a cousin of the late Queen Victoria, Lord Cecil, was converted to Christ. His life was dramatically changed. He now had a burning passion to share the Christ that had done so much for him with others. His one desire was to preach the gospel. He traveled to North America and spent much of his time in Canada. He shared the love of Christ everywhere he went—in large cities, in remote villages, among farmers, in the lumber camps, and in quiet seaside towns.

He told the story of one day passing a man's house that he knew was once a Christian but had seriously drifted away from Christ. He saw the man at his woodpile, industriously chopping wood for his cook stove. Knowing the man to be a backslider, one who had once been a faithful witness for his Savior but now was no longer attending church, Lord Cecil paused and shouted to him, "The Lord is coming, brother, the Lord is coming!" He said no more and continued walking.

The admonition, the Lord is coming, burned its way into this man's soul. These words reached the core of his being. Like a two-edged sword, they pierced his heart. His conscience smote him. They echoed again and again in his mind. "The Lord is coming." It seems he could not forget them. This urgent appeal from God's servant that the coming of the Lord was near so impressed this man that he recommitted his life to Christ and returned to church. Living in the light of the second coming of Christ influences your decisions and guides your choices—it is a powerful incentive to godly living. The apostle Peter understood this reality.

The aged warrior of the cross had come to the end of his life. His strength was ebbing away. He had been through the battle. His body was battered, bruised, and bloodied. Now he focused on the brevity of life.

The old man of God needed to speak. He could not keep silent. He had something to say of eternal significance. Listen to his words: "Yes, I think it is right, as long as I am in this tent, to stir you up by reminding you, knowing that shortly I must put off my tent, just as our Lord Jesus Christ showed me. Moreover, I will be careful to ensure that you always have a reminder of these things after my decease" (2 Peter 1:13–15).

The language here is remarkable. A tent is a temporary structure. It would remind Peter's Jewish Christian listeners of the wilderness wanderings of the Israelites for 40 years, when they dwelt in tents.

The root word for "decease" in Greek is the word "exodus." We are all on an exodus—a journey through a desert of time in the tentlike structures of our body. As believers we are pilgrims passing through this world on the way to glory when Jesus comes. We have a destination. We are not wandering mindlessly to nowhere.

If life is going nowhere, if there is not some end in sight, if we are drifting aimlessly along in the cosmos, life has no real meaning.

The epitaph on one of the heathen graves went something like this: "I was not, I was, now I am not, so eat, drink, and be merry, for soon you will be like me."

Shakespeare once defined life as "a tale told by an idiot, full of sound and fury, signifying nothing."

And some time ago a college newspaper ran a contest for the best definition of the word "life." Here is the entry that won: "Life is the penalty we pay for the crime of being born."

If there is nothing in life to live for but ultimate extinction at the end of our days, life has little meaning.

If all of life is moving to absolute nothingness, if time is a fleeting moment, if every breath takes us a closer step to oblivion, life becomes a cruel saga of pain, suffering, and injustice.

But the aged apostle breathes a breath of hope. Light pierces the darkness. Jesus is coming again.

Peter bases his conviction on two unchangeable facts: "For we did not follow cunningly devised fables when we made known to you the power and coming of our Lord Jesus Christ, but were eyewitnesses of His majesty" (verse 16).

"And so we have the prophetic Word confirmed, which you do well to heed as a light that shines in a dark place" (verse 19).

Here is Peter's reasoning for his certainty that Christ is coming:

1. **The Glory and Majesty of the Transfiguration**

Peter has beheld Christ's glory once. He has seen His majesty and power on the Mount of Transfiguration. This amazing mountain experience was a miniature of the second coming of our Lord. In the glorified Christ on the Mount of Transfiguration Peter beheld a powerful symbol of his glorified Lord returning in majesty.

In addition to the Transfiguration, Peter declares that the prophets through the ages have heralded the second coming of Christ.

2. **The Prophetic Word Speaks:**

  a. "Enoch, the seventh from Adam, prophesied . . . , saying, 'Behold, the Lord comes with ten thousands of His saints' " (Jude 14).

  b. David declared, "Our God shall come, and shall not keep silent" (Psalm 50:3).

  c. Isaiah cries out, "And the ransomed of the Lord shall . . . come to Zion with singing, with everlasting joy on their heads" (Isaiah 35:10).

  d. Daniel adds, "The God of heaven will set up a kingdom which shall never be destroyed" (Daniel 2:44).

  e. Ezekiel and Amos, Micah and Hosea, all shout it.

  f. Each of the Gospel writers, Matthew, Mark, Luke, and John, herald it.

g. The angels at Jesus' ascension declared, "This same Jesus, who was taken up from you into heaven, will so come in like manner as you saw Him go" (Acts 1:11).

h. Jesus Himself affirms this eternal truth echoed down through the ages by the prophets. "Let not your heart be troubled; you believe in God, believe also in Me. In My Father's house are many mansions; if it were not so, I would have told you. I go to prepare a place for you. And if I go and prepare a place for you, I will come again" (John 14:1–3).

Here is what Peter is saying: "Don't lose hope!" Echoing and reechoing down through the centuries are the voices of the prophets. They declare in trumpet tones that Jesus is coming again.

Many fail to understand that life on this planet will not go on forever. History is not an endless cycle of events moving in circles to nowhere. All of history is moving toward one grand, climactic event in the coming of Christ. As time passes and the second coming of Christ is delayed, there is a tendency to live as if His return made little difference at all. Peter addresses these issues in the second and third chapters of his second epistle, reminding us of the reality of Christ's return.

Christ's Coming Will Not Be Delayed Forever

In 2 Peter 2, Peter focuses on the reality of the coming judgment, but it is in chapter 3 that he takes on the scoffers and reveals the reason for the delay of the Advent. Every verse is filled with meaning, so we begin with "Beloved, I now write to you this second epistle (in both of which I stir up your pure minds by way of reminder), that you may be mindful of the words which were spoken before by the prophets" (2 Peter 3:1–3).

Peter will not let them forget. There is one prime reason for his letter: to keep the return of our Lord fresh in their minds. He continues with a scathing rebuke of the "scoffers." He warns against false teachers.

"Knowing this first that scoffers will come in the last days walking according to their own lusts and saying, 'Where is the promise of His coming? For since the fathers fell asleep, all things continue as they were from the beginning of creation' " (verse 4).

Peter's point is clear. The scoffers can scoff. The mockers can mock. The ridiculers can ridicule. The doubters can doubt. The skeptics can deny it, but that does not change the eternal truth one whit. Jesus is coming again, and that gives all life meaning.

Notice carefully what Peter says: "The scoffers are walking after their own lusts."

Often our morality dictates our beliefs. What you believe impacts how you live, and how you live impacts what you believe. Many a man, many a woman, reasons away divine truth because of some sin in their own life. If you are struggling with some divine truth, ask yourself this question: Is it because I do not understand? Is it more knowledge that I need? Or is there some long-cherished sin, some ingrained lifestyle practice, some questionable behavior, some deep-seated self-ish attitude, that I am reluctant to give up?

Often we plateau in our Christian experience, not because we need more knowledge, not because we don't know enough, not because we need to discover some amazing new revelation, but because there is some hidden sin, some long-cherished habit lurking deep within our lives. There are attitudes and practices not in harmony with God's will that require spiritual surgery, and sometimes surgery can be painful.

Why not ask God to speak to your heart and reveal un-childlike attitudes so you can be done with them in the name of Jesus? I pray that the Holy Spirit will reveal cherished sin so that we can surrender it. I pray that the Holy Spirit will be so powerfully present in our lives that we will see our sin, surrender our sins, and by the grace of Christ be overcomers.

There is an excellent definition of the holiness that Peter calls God's last-day people to: "Holiness is wholeness for God; It is the entire surrender of the heart and life to the indwelling of the principles of heaven" (Ellen G. White, *The Desire of Ages* [Mountain View, Calif.: Pacific Press® Pub. Assn., 1898, 1940], p. 556).

Does Jesus have every part of you and every fiber of your being? Are you Christ's and Christ's totally? Are you wholly sold out for God? In 2 Peter 3 the apostle is calling for radical discipleship. He is calling for a surrender far deeper than the scoffers are willing to go. Peter employs some powerful arguments against these scoffers. Here is what he says: "But, beloved, do not forget this one thing, that with the Lord one day is as a thousand years and a thousand years as one day" (verse 8).

"For this they willingly forget; that by the word of God the heavens were of old, and the earth standing out of water and in the water, by which the world that then existed perished, being flooded with water. But the heavens and earth which are now preserved by the same Word, are reserved for fire until the day of judgment and perdition of ungodly men" (verses 5–7).

The scoffers fail to understand two critical points.

1. They fail to understand God's view of time. His relationship to time is dramatically different than our relationship to time. God is never in a hurry. He is dealing with the great controversy in a way that His love, grace, and power will be revealed to the entire universe. His concern is for the security of the universe forever.
2. They fail to understand God's long-suffering, His patience, and His gracious kindness in desiring all humanity to be saved.

"The Lord is not slack concerning His promise, as some count slackness, but is longsuffering toward us, not willing that any should perish" (verse 9).

Why Jesus Waits

Have you ever wondered, "Why doesn't Jesus just come and put an end to all of this suffering?" Have you ever asked, "Why is Jesus waiting so long to complete the task? If He loves us, why doesn't He return soon and end this misery? How many more children must die of starvation before it is enough? How many more natural disasters or wars must take place before He says, 'It is finished'?"

The delay of the Advent is not because God is tardy. He is not slow to fulfill His promises. He is long-suffering. This long-suffering refers not only to God's gracious mercy and His patient longing to save all humanity. It also refers to His suffering. Sin causes God to suffer. The planet in rebellion brings sorrow to His heart.

He has endured the pain of sin for millenniums because in His great love He does not want one person lost. His heart is broken over sin. His capacity to suffer is directly proportionate to His capacity to love. His suffering began the day that sin began and will never end until the day that sin ends. He is the "Lamb slain from the foundation of the world" (Revelation 13:8).

As day by day Jesus sees the heartache and suffering in our world, His heart grieves. As Isaiah so aptly puts it: "In all their afflictions He was afflicted" (Isaiah 63:9).

The prophet Jeremiah asks, "Is it nothing to you, all you who pass by? Behold and see if there is any sorrow like my sorrow, which has been brought on me, which the Lord has inflicted in the day of His fierce anger" (Lamentations 1:12). Christ hung on Calvary's cross paying the ultimate price for the sins of all humanity, experiencing the full wrath of God against sin for you and me. As one writer states it: "The cross is a revelation to our dull senses of the pain that, from its very inception, sin has brought to the heart of God. Every departure from the right, every deed of cruelty, every failure of humanity to reach His ideal, brings grief to Him" (Ellen G. White, *Education* [Mountain View, Calif.: Pacific Press® Pub. Assn., 1903, 1952], p. 263).

The greatest motivation to turn loose of sin and rebellion is that it brings pain to the One who loves us so much.

The apostle now focuses the laser beam of truth on these last few verses in his concluding appeal. He makes an urgent, powerful call for us to be ready for the coming of our Lord. The aged apostle knows that his time is short. He recognizes that he does not have many opportunities left. His appeal is straight-forward and heartfelt. It rings with the assurance of our Lord's return.

"But the day of the Lord will come as a thief in the night, in which the heavens will pass away with a great noise, and the elements will melt with fervent heat. . . . Therefore, since all these things will be dissolved, what manner of persons ought you to be in holy conduct and godliness" (2 Peter 3:10, 11).

Peter's urgent appeal in the blazing light of the second coming of Christ is an appeal for holiness.

God has a problem: It's called the sin problem. Sin reigns in the universe, and it reigns in our hearts.

The central issue in the great controversy is over the character of God. Is the grip of grace greater than the grasp of sin? Is God's love more powerful then selfishness? Will there ever be a group of people in this world who love Jesus more than they love sin, whose hearts are more set on heaven than the things of this world, whose minds are fixed on eternity and who live totally dedicated, unselfish godly lives of service?

What can break the hold of sin on our lives? What can transform us into His image? What can deliver us from the chains of evil that bind us? What can release us from the prisons that so often enslave us? There is only one thing that has the power to do it, and that is the cross of Calvary.

Why is the cross the remedy for the sin problem? At the cross we see love in action. At the cross we see the divine, righteous Son of God, suffering in agony, pouring out His life for us.

At the cross we see the just dying for the unjust, the righteous One dying for the unrighteous, the innocent One dying for the guilty, the obedient One dying for the disobedient.

At the cross the divine Son of God bears the guilt, the weight, the burden, the shame, the condemnation, of our sin. We love Christ because He first loved us. When we really understand what He did for us on the cross, we are willing to commit our entire life to Him.

Shaken Out of Complacency

Peter's appeal shakes us out of our spiritual complacency.

Our Savior longs to do something in us so that He can do something through us.

He longs to do something for us so that He can do something with us.

He longs to change us, so that we can change the world.

We have only one life to live. Time is passing. Today is fading into tomorrow.

The past is rapidly becoming the present, and the present rushes into the future. In the floodlight of eternity, will you make that full, complete, absolute, total commitment— radical, all-out commitment to Jesus—that will change your life so that you can go out and change the world?

Recently my wife and I were in a small village in south central England. Etched in stone was this placard: "Every noble life leaves the fabric of it forever woven in the work of the world."

You have one life to live. What will you leave behind? What legacy will you leave? What will you weave into the fabric of this world? Will you live in the joyful light of the second coming of Christ? Will you leave this place filled with the hope of His return and go out with a new commitment to impact somebody for Christ?

Charles Studd grasped the significance of living a life with purpose. He had immersed his life in sports, seeking fame by playing on the English cricket team. In 1884, after his brother George was taken seriously ill, Charles was confronted by the question "What is all the fame and flattery worth when a man comes to face eternity?" He had to admit that since his conversion six years earlier he had been in "an unhappy, backslidden state." As a result of the experience he said, "I knew that cricket would not last, and honor would not last, and nothing in this world would last, but it was worthwhile living for the world to come."

Charles Studd responded to the invitation of Hudson Taylor and spent 15 years as a missionary in China, six years as a pastor in India, and more than 20 years in the heart of Africa sharing Christ in African villages where villagers had never heard the name of Christ. Pastor Studd summarized the purpose for living in that well-known poem "Only One Life, 'Twill Soon Be Past."

"Only one life, yes, only one,
Soon will its fleeting hours be done;
Then, in 'that day' my Lord to meet,

And stand before His Judgment seat;
Only one life, 'twill soon be past,
Only what's done for Christ will last. . . .

"When this bright world would tempt me sore,
When Satan would a victory score;
When self would seek its way,
Then help me, Lord, with joy to say:
Only one life, 'twill soon be past,
Only what's done for Christ will last."

Chapter 6

The Good News
of the Judgment

Daniel Webster was one of America's best-known statesmen and orators. His career of brilliant oratory and his ability to captivate audiences throughout early America made him one of the most popular speakers of his day.

On one occasion he was asked what he regarded as the greatest thought that ever occupied his mind. He replied: "The sense of my individual responsibility to God."

He went on to elaborate in these words . . .

"This thought is not pleasant to those who are living in their sins and out of relationship to Him, and consequently are not prepared to face the tremendous issues involved. But whether the issues are faced or not, the fact remains: 'So then every one of us shall give account of himself to God' [Romans 14:12, KJV]. We all *are* responsible to God, as the Word of God declares, and . . . cannot escape our responsibility."

Daniel Webster's words lead us to consider our choices carefully. Our character is formed as we establish repeated habit patterns as the result of the consistent daily choices we make. Choices are the stuff that life is made of, and our choices will determine our eternal destiny. God has created us with free will, and we are responsible for the choices we make. The judgment implies moral responsibility. It speaks to the fact that we are not mere machines or products of biological chance.

As Paul states: "For we must all appear before the judgment seat of Christ, that each one may receive the things done in the body, according what he has done, whether good or bad" (2 Corinthians 5:10). But the judgment is more—much, much more—than about us. It has to do with a universal struggle between good and evil. It focuses on an intergalactic cosmic battle for control of the universe.

God on Trial

The judgment is primarily about God. Is God fair? Is He just? Is He loving and merciful? In the great controversy that is raging in the universe, Lucifer, a rebel angel, has declared that God is an authoritarian tyrant. This fallen angel has defamed the character of God. He has portrayed God as selfish, desiring obedience and giving little in return. The evil one has claimed that God's laws restrict our happiness. He has charged God with the mismanagement of the universe. Don't misunderstand me!

There is no question that we are accountable to God.

There is no question that we are responsible for our actions.

There is no question that the decisions we make will determine our eternal destiny.

There is no question that we have free will and that our choices will determine our fate.

But in this chapter I want to share with you a larger picture and a broader understanding of the judgment that powerfully impacts our lives.

The Bible's last book, Revelation, is all about this war that

Satan has declared upon God. It is about this universal titanic struggle. Revelation focuses on the end of the agelong controversy between good and evil. Lucifer, a rebel angel, challenged the justice, fairness, and wisdom of God. He claimed that God is unfair and unjust in the way that He has administered the universe. At the very center of this conflict over the character of God is Revelation's final judgment. John states, "Then I saw another angel flying in the midst of heaven, having the everlasting gospel to preach . . . to every nation, tribe, tongue, and people—saying with a loud voice, 'Fear God and give glory to Him, for the hour of His judgment has come; and worship Him who made heaven and earth, the sea and springs of water' " (Revelation 14:6, 7).

Notice especially in the light of the everlasting gospel there is the expression "The hour of His judgment has come." This is the hour for the entire universe to see the goodness of our God. Once and for all the beings on unfallen worlds will see, in the light of the judgment hour, that God has done everything He can to save every human being.

There are three facts about Revelation's end-time judgment I want you to see clearly.

Fact 1: God's final judgment reveals God's justice and mercy. It says something about His love and law. It speaks of His grace to save and His power to deliver. It reveals to a waiting world and a watching universe His provisions to save all humanity.

The judgment is part of God's ultimate solution in the great controversy between good and evil in the universe. It answers the charges of Satan that God is unfair and unjust. When our names appear in judgment before God, Jesus will ask before the entire universe, "Could I have done anything more to save this individual?" Heaven's infinite, minute, exact, detailed records will be opened, and it will be shown once and for all time that there was nothing more Jesus Christ could have done to save us. The Father and Son have done everything possible to save this fallen planet. If we are lost, it is because of our deliberate choices to reject the love that longs for us to be saved eternally.

The entire universe and the unfallen worlds will see the countless times that God sent His Holy Spirit to our hearts. They will see the numberless times Jesus drew us to Him. They will then clearly understand how He sent angels to beat back the forces of Satan from our lives, how He arranged the circumstances in our lives so that we could get to know Him and how He revealed His majesty in the natural world to impress us with His goodness. Most of all they will understand more deeply the magnitude of His love in coming to this planet in rebellion, living the life we should have lived and dying the death we should have died. He took our place on the cross so we could share His throne in heaven.

All of this was for one purpose: to save us. In the final analysis every being in the universe will see that Calvary is enough, that the cross is sufficient. Jesus could do nothing more. He has done everything He could to redeem us. The entire universe will burst into rapturous song: "Great and marvelous are Your works. Just and true are Your ways, O King of the saints!" (Revelation 15:3).

Our choices reveal our response to the Holy Spirit's wooing on our hearts and His loving invitations to accept Him as our Savior and Lord. He is doing everything He can to save us. The judgment reveals our acceptance or rejection of His saving grace and power.

Revelation's judgment reveals God's unfathomable love as well as His justice in dealing with the controversy between good and evil. It reveals once and for all, now and forever, in the present and through all eternity, that heaven could not have done one more thing to save us. If there was anything more heaven could have done to save us, Jesus would have done it.

In the judgment before the unfallen beings in the universe, God reveals that He is both a God of amazing grace and eternal fairness.

There is a second aspect of this judgment in the heavenly courts above.

Fact 2: God's final judgment establishes Christ's throne forever. Throughout history God allowed sin to go on for only so long before His judgments fell. Although He has created us with the freedom of choice, He is sovereign. Our choices can never supersede His overall plan for this world. Sin and rebellion have their limits.

In the days just before the Flood, God appealed to humans through Noah for 120 years. Every person on earth had an opportunity to accept or reject Noah's message of warning. Once all were given ample opportunity to accept or reject heaven's message, the judgments of God fell as the rains came.

In the days of Sodom and Gomorrah, God appealed to those wicked cities through Abraham and Lot. Every inhabitant of those sin-cursed cities had an opportunity to accept God's grace, repent, and be saved. When the final warning had been given, the fire fell, and God's judgments devastated Sodom and Gomorrah.

In the days of ancient Babylon, God sent His witness Daniel to that heathen nation. Daniel lived in Babylon as a captive for more than 70 years. Day by day he witnessed God's way of life to the Babylonians. Eventually Babylon finally and fully rejected God's invitation to accept His ways. Eventually Babylon reached the height of its rebellion against God under the young King Belshazzar. The Scriptures declare of the Babylonian king, "But you his son, Belshazzar, have not humbled your heart, although you knew all this" (Daniel 5:22).

Babylon knew but did not do. Our great sin is not that we do not know—it is that we do not do what we know. Our great sin is not ignorance, but the human heart's rebellion against the divine principles of heaven.

In his book *Authentic Christianity*, John Stott puts it this way: "We need to repent of the haughty way in which we sometimes stand in judgment upon Scripture and must learn to sit humbly under its judgments instead. If we come to Scripture with our minds made up, expecting to hear from it only an echo of our own thoughts and never the thunderclap of God's, then indeed he will not speak to us and we shall only be confirmed in our own prejudices. We must allow the Word of God to confront us, to disturb our security, to undermine our complacency and to overthrow our patterns of thought and behavior."

When was the last time you were confronted by something in the Word of God?

When was the last time that the Word of God disturbed your security?

When was the last time the Word of God shook you out of your complacency?

When was the last time you read something in Scripture and said, "I really need to make a change in my life"?

The Bible commentator William Barclay puts it this way: "The difference between the cynic and the Christian is this. The cynic judges the Word of God. Christians allow the Word to judge them."

When was the last time that the Holy Spirit convicted you of some sin in your life so dramatically that you knew you had to make a change? that the conviction of the Spirit was so great that you could not resist any longer?

Babylon was a thrill-jaded, pleasure-centered society worshipping the idols of their own making and turned away from the true God. Its immorality and drunkenness dominated its culture. It worshipped the gods of its invention and exalted its so-called wisdom above God's divine Revelation.

Are the seeds of Babylon's fall sprouting in America today? Is the handwriting on the wall? Are God's judgments soon to fall on a society that is rapidly repudiating the values of the Almighty?

In a speech made in 1863 Abraham Lincoln said: "We have been the recipients of the choicest bounties of Heaven; we have been preserved these many years in peace and prosperity; we have grown in numbers, wealth, and power as no other nation has ever grown. But we have forgotten God. We have forgotten the gracious hand which preserved us in peace and multiplied and enriched and strengthened us, and we have vainly imagined, in the deceitfulness of our hearts, that all these blessings were produced by some superior wisdom and virtue of our own. Intoxicated with unbroken success, we have become too self-sufficient to feel the necessity of redeeming and preserving grace, too proud to pray to the God that made us."

Daniel Webster, statesman and scholar, adds: "If we abide by the principles taught in the Bible, our country will . . . prosper; but if we and our posterity neglect its instructions and authority, no man can tell how sudden a catastrophe may overwhelm us and bury our glory in profound obscurity."

The sinful civilizations of the past were all given an opportunity to repent; but when they rejected God's mercy, spurned His love and turned their backs on His grace, eventually the judgments of God fell. Babylon, Media-Persia, Greece, and Rome all filled their cup of iniquity, and at God's appointed time in the timetable of heaven His judgments fell.

In a wonderful commentary on the Old Testament we read this: "With unerring accuracy the Infinite One still keeps account with the nations. While His mercy is tendered, with calls to repentance, this account remains open; but when the figures reach a certain amount which God has fixed, the ministry of His wrath begins. The account is closed. Divine patience ceases. Mercy no longer pleads in their behalf" (Ellen G. White, *Prophets and Kings* [Mountain View, Calif.: Pacific Press® Pub. Assn., 1917], p. 364).

God is merciful. He always sends a message of warning and repentance before His judgments fall. Before His final judgment, He sends the message of the everlasting gospel to the ends of the earth. Every person on the planet will have their final opportunity to accept the truths of His Word and prepare for His soon return. Once this final message is rapidly proclaimed to all earth's peoples, the decree will go forth: "He who is unjust, let him be unjust still; he who is filthy, let him be filthy still; he who is righteous, let him be righteous still; he who is holy, let him be holy still. And behold, I am coming quickly, and My reward is with Me" (Revelation 22:11, 12). Our choices will determine our eternal destiny. God has done everything possible to save us. Soon the judgments of God will fall upon this earth, and the wicked forces of evil will be destroyed forever.

Revelation's Babylon Destroyed

Throughout Scripture Babylon represents the oppressor of God's people. It is the citadel of error. The center of apostasy It stands for rebellion against God and disobedience to the divine commands. God's judgments on Old Testament Babylon represent the final judgments upon this world. The story of Babylon's fall is instructive to an end-time people. You will recall that Babylon had attacked Jerusalem and took many of the Israelites, including Daniel, into captivity. Cyrus, the Persian king of the East, attacked Babylon and freed the Jewish captives and allowed them to return to Jerusalem and worship the true God.

Once again at the time of the end, God's people will be oppressed and persecuted by a religious oppressor called Babylon the Great (Revelation 17:5). The book of Revelation predicts that at a time of social chaos, political crisis, natural disasters, and economic collapse, Jesus will return to triumph over the oppressive powers of this world and liberate His people. He will reign forever. He will establish His throne securely in the universe forever. In the battle for the throne He will be victor. His people will journey with Him through the corridors of time and limitless space to worship in the New Jerusalem.

If ever there was a time to be sure our lives are right with Jesus, that time is today. If ever there was a time to be sure that there is nothing between our souls and our Savior, that time is today. If ever there was a time to be certain about our salvation in Christ, that time is today. We are living on the knife edge of eternity; this is no time for playing religious games. This is no time for make-believe Christianity. The call of the judgment hour is the call for a total commitment of our lives to Christ.

Statesman Daniel Webster's Commitment

Another incident in statesman Daniel Webster's life gives testimony to the depth of his commitment and his faith in the Lord Jesus Christ. During a summer holiday in a district far away from the capital, he went to a little country church service each Sunday.

His niece asked him why he went there, when the preachers in Washington, D.C., were far more learned and eloquent, and why he paid little attention to far abler sermons. "In Washington," he replied, "they preach to Daniel Webster the statesman. But this man has been talking to Daniel Webster the sinner, and telling him of Jesus."

Webster knew he needed his faith to be challenged, and he welcomed the opportunity to keep growing in Jesus.

God has given the freedom of choice to each one of us. Day by day He appeals to us to accept the salvation He so freely offers. The judgment reveals both His goodness and our choices. It reveals how much He desires to save us and whether we desire to be saved as much as He desires it. The judgment reveals how much He wants us to be in heaven with Him and whether we want to be there as much as He wants us there.

The way of Babylon is the way of this world. When this world has more of an attraction in our lives than heaven, something is tragically wrong. When the pleasures and immorality of Babylon have a greater grip upon us than His grace, something is tragically wrong. When the falsehoods and deceptions of Babylon influence our thinking and overshadow the truth of God's Word, something is tragically wrong.

Fact 3: God's final judgment reveals the saving righteousness of Jesus and His triumph over Satan and the powers of hell.

There is a wonderful description of the judgment in Revelation 4 and 5. The apostle John writes: "After these things I looked, and behold, a door standing open in heaven. And the . . . voice which I heard was . . . saying, 'Come up here, and I will show you things which must take place after this' " (Revelation 4:1). Jesus invites us to look through the open door into heaven's sanctuary to view eternal scenes in the great controversy between good and evil.

What do we see when we look through heaven's open door? What do we hear as we bend our ears heavenward? What scene captures the attention of the entire heavenly host? We see a throne set in heaven (verse 2). God sits upon His throne as the rightful ruler of the universe. The scene is one of the enthronement of Christ after His resurrection and ascension to heaven. The rainbow around the throne reveals God's justice and mercy. His love and His law.

There are 24 elders around the throne (verse 4). Who are these 24 elders that gather around the throne? They are men and women of all ages resurrected at the time of Christ's resurrection and ascended to heaven with Him (Matthew 27:52; Ephesians 4:7). This is good news. There are some redeemed from the earth who are around the throne of God. They faced temptations, just as we face them. They experienced the same challenges in life that we face and were confronted with similar problems, but in every generation there have been those who have overcome. Through the grace of Christ and the power of the living God they overcame the power temptations of Satan. They are clothed in "white robes," signifying the righteousness of Christ that covers and cleanses their sins.

John's eyes then focus on four living creatures at God's throne. Who are the four living creatures in Revelation 4:6, 7? Israel marched in the wilderness under four banners: a lion, a calf, the face of a man, and a flying eagle. These banners indicated God's continual protection and everlasting guidance. Jesus, the lion of the tribe of Judah, left the glories of heaven and in becoming a man accepted the role of a sacrificial animal, the calf, but was resurrected to His Father's throne, the eagle.

These four living creatures represent the offering of praise that all of heaven will give to Jesus throughout the ceaseless ages for His sacrificial love. They represent the beings on every unfallen world, all the heavenly beings and all the redeemed.

This crescendo of praise leads to a hymn of highest praise: "You are worthy, O Lord, to receive glory and honor and power; for You created all things, and by Your will they exist and were created" (Revelation 4:11). Jesus is our Creator, our Redeemer, and our coming King. The One who created us has redeemed us and is coming again for us. Revelation 4 is the prelude to Revelation 5.

In John's vision of the throne room of the universe we see a scroll in the hand of the everlasting Father. This unusual scroll is written on both sides.

An angel steps forward and in a loud voice asks, "Who is worthy to open the scroll?" (Revelation 5:2). The fate of the entire human race is recorded upon this scroll. The destiny of millions is to be decided. The issues are serious. It appears that there is no one in heaven that can represent humanity before the throne of God. The scroll obviously contains the eternal records of all humankind.

All of heaven is silent. Then the sound of weeping is heard. Can anyone open the scroll? Will humans be doomed forever? But wait, there is One who steps forth. Revelation 5:5 records this amazing scene. One of the heavenly beings steps forth and speaks. John declares: "But one of the elders said to me, 'Do not weep. Behold, the Lion of the tribe of Judah, the Root of David, has prevailed to open the scroll. . . .' And I looked, and behold, . . . a Lamb as though it had been slain" (verses 5, 6).

As Jesus, the Lamb of God who has sacrificed His life for the salvation of all humanity, takes the scroll of judgment and opens it, all of heaven bursts forth in rapturous praise. They sing a new song of eternal praise.

"You are worthy to take the scroll, and to open its seals; for You were slain, and have redeemed us to God by Your blood out of every tribe and tongue and people and nation, and have made us kings and priests to our God; and we shall reign on the earth" (verses 9, 10).

The living Christ stands for us in the judgment, and before the whole universe declares we are His. He is for us. His wounded hands are enough. His pierced side is enough. The cross of Calvary is enough. We can face the judgment with confidence when we face it with Him.

Daniel's Vision of the Judgment

There is a parallel scene in Daniel 7. Babylon, Media-Persia, Greece, and Rome rise and oppress the people of God. A religio-political power rising out of Rome counterfeits the truth of God and persecutes the people of God during the Middle Ages.

Daniel's attention is then drawn from earth to heaven, where God's judgment sits. The prophet states, "I watched till thrones were put in place, and the Ancient of Days was seated; His garment was white as snow, and the hair of His head was like pure wool. His throne was a fiery flame. . . . A thousand thousand ministered to Him; ten thousand times ten thousand stood before Him. The court [judgment] was seated, and the books were opened" (Daniel 7:9, 10). Tens of thousands of heavenly beings assemble around the throne of God. The Son of man, Jesus Christ, comes to the Ancient of Days (verse 13). Judgment is made in favor of the people of God.

In Christ, through Christ, because of Christ, they are exonerated before the universe. His sacrifice is sufficient. His perfect life atones for their imperfect lives. His death substitutes for their eternal death. As one author so aptly put it: He "was treated as we deserve, that we might be treated as He deserves. . . . He suffered the death which was ours, that we might receive the life which was His" (Ellen G. White, *The Desire of Ages* [Mountain View, Calif.: Pacific Press® Pub.

Assn., 1898, 1940], p. 25). In the final judgment Satan and all his evil forces are condemned. Their final destruction is certain. Jesus receives the kingdom and gives it to His faithful followers (verses 26, 27). He will reign forever and ever. His throne is secure. His kingdom has prevailed. Evil has been vanquished.

The heavenly beings are looking forward to this final judgment. The eternal questions asked before the entire universe are those questions we all ask at times. Is there anyone that can take away our guilt? Who can forgive our sins? Where can we find the power to overcome the temptations that so often trip us up? Is eternal life possible? Will evil reign forever? When will sin be finally and fully done away with? The judgment provides the answer. Jesus, the divine Son of God, is worthy to open the scrolls of judgment. In Him we have salvation full and complete.

We need not fear. Jesus stands for us in the judgment, and the powers of hell are defeated. Through the ceaseless ages of eternity we sing the praises and glory of Jesus. He redeemed us. He shed His blood for us. He sacrificed His life for us. He is our Savior, our Redeemer, our slain Lamb, our interceding High Priest, our living Christ. Christ is all we need and everything our heart desires. We need not fear the judgment—it is good news. The good news that His grace is sufficient. The good news that His power is greater than the powers of evil. The good news that Satan will no more have dominion over us. The good news that evil is gone forever. The good news that Jesus will reign forever, and we too can reign with Him forever.

Chapter 7

Powerful Winds Are Blowing

The arms race is back. In 2015 the United States spent $598.5 billion to ramp up its military. Since 1945 the United States has produced more than 70,000 nuclear warheads. Russia continues to produce nuclear weapons at a frightening pace. China and Iran have joined the nuclear club. The threat of an all-out nuclear war continues at an alarming rate. North Korea has tested a new type of intercontinental ballistic missile, topped with a "super-large heavy warhead," which can strike the U.S. mainland. According to the projections, the missile, armed with a nuclear warhead, could reach Los Angeles in 38 minutes, Chicago in about 45 minutes, and New York and Washington, D.C., within an hour.

North Korea's state media made the announcement of the missile test just hours after leader Kim Jong-un ordered the 3:00 a.m. launch of the Hwasong-15 missile, which reached the highest altitude ever recorded by a North Korean missile.

State news agency KCNA called its so-called new missile "the most powerful ICBM" and said that it "meets the goal of the completion of the rocket weaponry system development."

After the launch, Kim said North Korea had "finally realized the great historic cause of completing the state nuclear force," according to KCNA.

U.S. Defense secretary James Mattis said earlier that the

missile launched demonstrated that North Korea had the ability to hit "everywhere in the world."

For millions it is extremely frightening that human leaders in several nations can plunge the world into a nuclear war with merely the push of a button. It appears they are now able to fire a missile with a nuclear warhead and hit any major city in the world.

Jesus was truly right when He warned in Luke 21:26: ". . . men's hearts failing them from fear and the expectation of those things which are coming on the earth, for the powers of the heavens will be shaken. Then they will see the Son of Man coming in a cloud with power and great glory. Now when these things begin to happen, look up and lift up your heads, because your redemption draws nigh."

The Devastating Effects of Nuclear War

For the first time in history the human race has the capacity, the capability, of destroying itself. Nuclear annihilation is possible. What would the effects of a limited nuclear strike be? The United States Senate Committee on Foreign Relations commissioned a scientific study on the effects of nuclear war. Scientists from some of America's most prestigious universities were involved. Here is their conclusion: "In addition to the tens of millions of deaths during the days and weeks after the attack, there would probably be further millions (perhaps further tens of millions) of deaths in the ensuing months or years. In addition to the enormous economic destruction caused by the actual nuclear explosions, there would be some years during which the residual economy would decline further, as stocks (supplies) were consumed and machines wore out faster than recovered production could replace them. Nobody knows how to estimate the likelihood that industrial civilization might collapse in the areas attacked; additionally, the possibility of significant long-term ecological damage strongly exists."

Without the divine perspective, things can look grim. They can be downright scary; that's why Jesus declared that "men's hearts" would be "failing them from fear." Emotional stress is one of the leading reasons for coronary heart disease today. People are stressed out regarding the future. They are uncertain about what is coming. They do not know what to expect.

Facing the Future With Confidence

Looking 2,000 years into the future, John the revelator forecast the possibility of world annihilation that we are witnessing before our eyes today. But there is one major difference: John reveals hope for today, tomorrow, and forever.

"Then the seventh angel sounded: And there were loud voices in heaven, saying, 'The kingdoms of this world have become the kingdoms of our Lord and of His Christ, and He shall reign for ever and ever!' And the twenty-four elders who sat before God on their thrones fell on their faces and worshiped God, saying, 'We give You thanks, O Lord God Almighty, the One who is and who was and who is to come, because You have taken Your great power and reigned. The nations were angry, and Your wrath has come, and the time of the dead, that they should be judged, and that You should reward Your servants the prophets and the saints, and those who fear Your name, small and great, and should destroy those who destroy the earth' " (Revelation 11:15–18).

The nations of this world tremble and shake before the living Christ. Despotic world leaders will not destroy this world warring against one another in some nuclear holocaust. The earth trembles. Human beings quake in fear. Nuclear war looms, but our Lord is in control. There is hope on the horizon.

God will have the final word. He will make the final move. The winds of the Spirit will blow across this world, and the light of heaven's truth will be proclaimed to every nation, language, tribe, and people. Tens of thousands who have never heard the gospel will respond to the Word of God. Heaven is preparing the greatest spiritual revival in the history of our world. At a time of unusual crises God is preparing to do something amazing, and you and I can be a part of it. And that is what I want to share with you in this chapter.

The Holy Spirit is about to do something remarkable in our world, and is even now doing something remarkable, and we do not want to miss it.

There are two aspects I will share regarding this mighty move of God in earth's final hours. The first is what the mighty winds of the Holy Spirit want to do in us, and second, what the Spirit wants to do through us. Here are two very familiar passages about the "winds of the Spirit." It is my prayer that the Spirit will touch your heart and powerfully move in your life as you read these pages. Reading this chapter may be one of the most significant moments of your life. As you read, ask God to open your heart to the moving of the Holy Spirit. Ask Him to impress His will upon your heart deeply.

The Spirit cannot do much with us until first He has done

something for us. He cannot do much through us until He does something to us.

The Story of Nicodemus

Who was this Nicodemus that came to Jesus by night? We know that he must have been very wealthy. When Jesus died, Nicodemus brought, according to John's Gospel, "a mixture of myrrh and aloes, about a hundred pounds," to anoint His body (John 19:39). Only a very wealthy man could have brought that expensive anointing mixture. Nicodemus was well respected and came from an extremely aristocratic family. He was well known in Jerusalem.

He was a Pharisee. In many ways the Pharisees were the best people in the whole country. There were only about 6,000 of them in all of Israel. They took a solemn oath to spend their lives in meticulous obedience to every aspect of the Jewish law. Here was their basic understanding of the Law, or the first five books of the Bible.

"The Law is complete; it contains everything necessary for living a good life; therefore in the Law there must be a rule and a regulation to govern every possible incident in every possible moment of life for every possible man."

Nicodemus was also a member of the Sanhedrin. The Sanhedrin was the supreme court of the Jews and consisted of 71 members. He was a tithe-paying, Sabbathkeeping, health-reforming Jew looking forward to the coming of the Messiah, but there was something else about Nicodemus worthy of our notice.

Nicodemus was a puzzled man. He had all the outward appearances of religion, but something was dramatically missing.

The external trappings did not satisfy his heart needs. There was an aching of the soul deep down within. It happened then, and it happens now. Often what we see on the outside is really not what's happening on the inside. Often what appears to be is not. The cloak of religion does not meet our heart needs. He was unsatisfied with what he had, and longed for more. There was a hidden hunger, an insatiable thirst, that all of the religious practices of Judaism did not satisfy.

Religiosity is never a substitute for spirituality. Nicodemus came at night to find the light. He came in the darkness to discover the dawn of a new day. He came in secret, but one day would witness in public.

Addressing Jesus, he said, "Rabbi, we know that You are a teacher come from God" (John 3:2). Sensing his need, understanding his inner longing, Jesus ignored his comment and appealed directly to his heart.

"Jesus answered and said to him, 'Most assuredly, I say to you, unless one is born again, he cannot see the kingdom of God' " (verse 3).

Nicodemus was astounded. He did not really understand Jesus' words, so he asked, "How can a man be born when he is old? Can he enter a second time into his mother's womb and be born?" (verse 4). William Barclay puts Nicodemus' question this way:

"You talk about being born anew; you talk about this radical, fundamental change which is so necessary. I know that it is necessary; but in my experience it is impossible. There is nothing I would like more; but you might as well tell me, a full grown man, to enter my mother's womb and be born all over again" (William Barclay, *Gospel of John*,

Barclay's Bible Commentary, vol. 1, p. 114).

It was not the desirability of this change that Nicodemus questioned, but the possibility of the change. He knew he needed a change of heart, but was powerless to accomplish it. He knew something was missing. He knew he needed some kind of radical transformation. He wanted a change, longed for a change, but could not change himself.

Maybe you too have felt like Nicodemus. You have the outer trappings of religion, but something is missing inside. There is a longing within your heart to go deeper, but you struggle with whether it is possible or not. Or possibly you are not religious at all, yet like Nicodemus there is this aching longing within. You desire something more in life and are uncertain what it is. You have this void inside that nothing seems to really satisfy.

It was at this point that Jesus introduced the greatest source of power in the universe. "Most assuredly, I say to you, unless one is born of water and the Spirit, he cannot enter the kingdom of God" (verse 5). Water is a symbol of cleansing. The Spirit is a symbol of power.

Jesus continued: "That which is born of the flesh is flesh, and that which is born of the Spirit is spirit. Do not marvel that I said to you, 'You must be born again.' The wind blows where it wishes, and you hear the sound of it, but cannot tell where it comes from and where it goes. So is everyone who is born of the Spirit" (verse 6).

Let's look at this passage carefully. Jesus laid down a great law of human nature. Left alone without divine aid, we are flesh, and struggle with frustrated defeat. We may desire to do right, but have no power to carry out our desires. Left alone, we are powerless. In our sinful condition with our hereditary and cultivated tendencies toward sin, we cannot overcome without divine aid. This is a universal fact of human nature.

Lives Transformed by Grace

But according to Jesus, victory is possible. Our lives can be radically transformed. We can find meaning and deep purpose in life as well as the power to change. When the third person of the Godhead, the Holy Spirit, enters our lives, He is the essence of divine power. When the Holy Spirit blows like the wind upon the heart and life of the believer, frustrated defeat becomes glorious victory.

The wind of the Spirit blew upon the disciples:
- James and John, the sons of thunder, became the apostles of love.
- Thomas, the one who was consumed with doubt, was now filled with faith.
- Weak, vacillating Peter became steadfast and courageous.

The wind of the Spirit blew upon some Jewish outcasts:
- A scheming businessman named Simon, filled with emptiness and longing for a new life, was touched by the presence of the living Christ.
- Two demon-possessed men were delivered and became the first Christian missionaries.
- An attractive young woman soiled her moral purity but was transformed by grace. Mary was the last at the cross and the first at the tomb. She became a

powerful witness to the redemptive love of Christ.

The wind of the Spirit blew upon
- An African farmer called Simon, who joyfully carried Christ's cross in the face of ridicule and mockery up Golgotha's mountain.
- A young rebel whose life had gone tragically wrong. He hung on a cross beside Jesus, and in an instant his life was changed.
- A calloused Roman centurion who had his hard heart changed at the cross. He witnessed the miracle of love, and his life was never the same again.
- An ardent, devoted persecutor of the Christians, and the persecutor Saul was changed to the mighty apostle and evangelist Paul.

The Holy Spirit is still working miracles of divine grace in human hearts. What we can never accomplish of ourselves He can accomplish in us. What is impossible for us is possible for Him. The wind of the Spirit is powerful. It is life-changing. It is regenerating. The apostle Paul makes this powerful statement: "Therefore, if anyone is in Christ, he is a new creation; old things have passed away; behold, all things have become new" (2 Corinthians 5:17). In Christ we become a "new creation." The same Holy Spirit that worked so actively at the original Creation to bring life to this world creates new life in everyone who opens their heart to His life-changing power.

The apostle Paul then adds these reassuring words: "But when the kindness and the love of God our Savior toward man appeared, not by works of righteousness which we have done, but according to His mercy He saved us, through the washing of regeneration and the renewing of the Holy Spirit" (Titus 3:4, 5).

Regeneration goes down to the depths of the inmost soul, transforming our thoughts, realigning our affections, redirecting our will, and changing our actions.

Writing to believers at Ephesus, who were living in the midst of a decadent and corrupt society, Paul wants them to know "what is the exceeding greatness of His power toward us who believe, according to the working of His mighty power which He worked in Christ when He raised Him from the dead" (Ephesians 1:19).

Christianity is not merely accepting a set of beliefs and vainly struggling to live up to them. It is not gritting our teeth and saying, "I am going to do this if it kills me." It is so falling in love with the Christ who redeemed us on Calvary's cross that we allow Him through His Holy Spirit to transform our lives.

The Holy Spirit is Christ's most precious gift to you and me. Jesus longs for the winds of the Spirit to blow upon your life and mine and change them, radically change them, to be conformed to His image.

According to Scripture

For some people the Holy Spirit is very illusive. It is difficult for them to comprehend who He is. According to the Bible the Holy Spirit is the third person of the Godhead. The Scriptures speak a lot more about what He does than His nature. Here are just a few things the Bible says about Him.

The Holy Spirit is the "Spirit of life" (Romans 8:2).

The Holy Spirit is the Spirit "of power and of love" (2 Timothy 1:7).

The Holy Spirit is the "Spirit of grace" (Hebrews 10:29).

The Holy Spirit is the "Spirit of truth" (John 14:17).

The Holy Spirit is the "Spirit of glory" (1 Peter 4:14).

The Holy Spirit convicts us of sin, teaches us the ways of God, and reveals the beauty of Jesus to our longing souls (John 16:7, 8, 13, 14).

The Holy Spirit changes our hearts, strengthens our wills, and reveals divine truth to us.

The presence of the Holy Spirit is indispensable in our lives if we are to grow in grace and have the power to reach the world.

One of the most enlightening and spiritually penetrating books on the life of Christ is a book titled *The Desire of Ages*. Here is a remarkable statement on page 671.

"The Holy Spirit was the highest of all gifts that He [Jesus] could solicit from His Father for the exaltation of His people. The Spirit was to be given as a regenerating agent, and without this the sacrifice of Christ would have been of no avail. The power of evil had been strengthening for centuries, and the submission of men to this satanic captivity was amazing. Sin could be resisted and overcome only through the mighty agency of the Third Person of the Godhead, who would come with no modified energy, but in the fullness of divine power. It is the Spirit that makes effectual what has been wrought out by the world's Redeemer. It is by the Spirit that the heart is made pure. Through the Spirit the believer becomes a partaker of the divine nature. Christ has given His Spirit as a divine power to overcome all hereditary and cultivated tendencies to evil, and to impress His own character upon His church."

It is through the power of the Holy Spirit that an entire change can be made in our lives. It is through the power of the Holy Spirit that we are able to overcome "all" weaknesses, drives, and inclinations inherited through the corrupt stream of human nature passed down through our genetic line, and those sins we have cultivated through our personal repeated choices. This is the good news of the gospel. Jesus delivers us from the penalty of sin and the power of sin. If this is not true, then the gospel has little power. It becomes only a legal transaction to provide pardon; but Jesus offers us more. We need freedom from guilt, but we need much more. We need the Holy Spirit to transform our lives. This is exactly what Jesus offers us. He has promised the Holy Spirit to radically transform our lives. But there is even more.

Pentecost Repeated

It is through the power of the Holy Spirit that the gospel will be proclaimed rapidly to the world. It happened in the first century, and it will happen again. It happened at Pentecost for the New Testament church, and it will happen again for Christ's last-day people. It happened then and there, and it can happen here and now.

Let's go back to the first century and review again the experience of these New Testament believers when a mighty wind blew.

The mission before them seemed impossible. The task appeared overwhelming. The first-century Roman world was a corrupt, immoral, materialistic society. Jesus encouraged this small band of believers with the promise of the Holy Spirit.

He said, "It is not for you to know the times or seasons which the Father has put in His own authority. But you shall receive power when the Holy Spirit has come upon you; and you shall be witnesses to Me in Jerusalem, and in all Judea and Samaria, and to the end of the earth" (Acts 1:7, 8).

In other words: "Do not be so concerned about the exact time of My return that you miss what is essential: opening your heart to the ministry of the Spirit and receiving His power so that you can change the world."

The disciples obeyed the command of Christ. They prayed. They confessed their sins. One ambition swallowed up all others, one desire filled their minds, one goal dominated their lives—people won to Christ and saved in His kingdom.

And God answered their united prayers. The book of Acts is the story of the triumph of the gospel. Let your own heart thrill as you catch the amazing progress of Christianity in the first century.

"When the Day of Pentecost had fully come, they were all with one accord in one place. And suddenly there came a sound from heaven, as of a mighty rushing wind, and it filled the whole house where they were sitting" (Acts 2:1, 2).

In Acts 2 we read that 3,000 people were baptized in one day. In Acts 4 another 5,000 men were added, besides women and children. Acts 6 adds that "the word of God spread, and the number of the disciples multiplied greatly in Jerusalem" (Acts 2:41, 4:4; 6:7). The outpouring of the Spirit is likened to a mighty rushing wind that blows through the land. The Spirit touches hearts. Minds are opened. Truth clear as the noonday sun shines into darkened minds.

The disciples' fear was gone. It danced away like a fading

shadow. The dark night of gloom was over. Morning had come. Faith filled their hearts. The mighty outpouring of the Holy Spirit on Pentecost launched the Christian church with power. The challenge of reaching the world with the gospel seemed impossible.

These early believers did not have mass media, radio, television, or the Internet. They did not have the social media network, such as Facebook, Twitter, or text messaging. They did not have a satellite network of television stations. They did not have seminaries, educational institutions, hospitals, and publishing houses, but this they had: the fullness of the Holy Spirit. A mighty rushing wind blew across the land, and tens of thousands of believers flocked to the church in a few short decades.

The Mighty Outpouring of the Holy Spirit Will Come Again

The same Holy Spirit that was poured out on the New Testament believers to launch the church in Acts will be poured out more abundantly in latter-rain power to finish the work of God on earth.

Here is an amazing prophecy in Revelation 18:1: "After these things I saw another angel coming down from heaven, having great authority and the earth was illuminated with his glory."

God did the impossible in the first century, and He will do it again. The Holy Spirit moved powerfully then, and He will do it again. You can be a witness of His love to your world in these critical hours of world history. People are seeking, looking, desiring, longing for something substantial to cling to. There is a sense of uncertainty about the future, a sense that something is about to happen, but people wonder what it is. There is a feeling of anxiety in the air.

God is opening doors for the proclamation of the gospel around the world. Nations once closed are miraculously opening. Through the Internet, satellite radio, television, and a variety of other means God is reaching people with His message of Bible truth for this hour of earth's history. Something remarkable is happening, and you can be a part of it. He will open doors for you to share the gospel with others.

The most effective way to reach others with the gospel is to let God change your own heart. When He does something for us, He can do something with us. There is not greater satisfaction and joy than seeing others find life's deeper purpose through Christ.

It is my prayer that the Holy Spirit will so transform your life that you will discover the joy of sharing Jesus' love and grace with others. Soon the earth will be lightened with the glory of God. Soon the knowledge of His Word will go to the ends of the earth. Soon, very soon, every person will make their final decision for or against Christ. Soon the final call will be given and soon Jesus will come. I pray that the sparks of revival will kindle a flame in our hearts so that we can burn brightly for the glory of God.

Would you like to say, "Jesus, I want to recommit my life to You today, asking You to fill me with Your Holy Spirit so that I can be a mighty witness for You in the closing work"?

Chapter 8

The Nations Shall Hear

One of the more significant events of World War I was the sinking of the Cunard ocean liner R.M.S. *Lusitania.* Germany waged submarine warfare against the United Kingdom. The British Royal Navy had blockaded Germany to cut off the German supply lines. The *Lusitania* was identified and torpedoed by the German U-boat *U-20* on Friday, May 7, 1915, and sank in 18 minutes. The vessel went down 11 miles off the Old Head of Kinsale, Ireland, killing 1,198 and leaving 763 survivors. The sinking turned the tide of public opinion in many countries against Germany, contributed to the American entry into World War I, and, in military recruiting campaigns, became an iconic symbol of why the war was being fought.

There is a story attached to this disaster that has relevance to Bible-believing Christians living in the last days of human history. Lord Joseph Duveen was the American head of a prestigious art firm in the United States. In 1915 he planned to send one of his experts to England to examine some ancient pottery. He booked him a passage on the *Lusitania.* The German embassy issued a warning that the ocean liner might be torpedoed. Lord Duveen wanted to call off the trip. "I can't take the risk of your being killed," he said to his young pottery expert.

"Don't worry," the young man replied. "I am a strong swimmer, and when I read what was happening in the Atlantic, I began hardening myself by spending time every day in a tub of ice. At first I could stand it for only a few minutes, but this morning I stayed in that tub for nearly two hours."

Naturally Lord Duveen laughed. It sounded preposterous. But this daring young man sailed, and the *Lusitania* was torpedoed. The amazing thing is that the young man was rescued after five hours in the chilly waters and was still in excellent condition.

He had prepared himself in advance for the tough times that were coming. In His sermon on end-time events in Matthew 24, Jesus gives three admonitions to prepare ahead of time for His return. In verse 4 He states, "Take heed that no one deceives you." In other words: "Be on guard." In verse 42 He adds: "Watch therefore, for you do not know what hour your Lord is coming." In other words, stay alert to the signs that are taking place all around you. And third, our Lord declares in verse 44, "You also be ready, for the Son of Man is coming at an hour you do not expect." It would be more accurate to translate the passage this way: "Be in a state of readiness." Jesus does not say, "Get ready." He says, "Be ready."

Our world is filled with uncertainty. In many respects the future appears grim. Scientists warn of global warming that is melting the polar ice caps and can threaten thousands of coastal cities with flooding. Natural disasters are increasing. Hurricanes, tornadoes, wild forest fires, and earthquakes are becoming commonplace. Violent crime is rapidly rising. Our cities have become unsafe. And this crime surge is not only in the inner city. White-collar crime by company executives is becoming all too frequent.

The economy of the Western world teeters on a slender thread between prosperity and poverty. Nuclear weapons are in the hands of more nations than ever before and pose a growing threat. Morality wanes. Moral values that used to be the foundation of our society have been washed away like a sandcastle before a mighty, rushing ocean wave. For most people life continues as normal. There is little consciousness that we are living on the verge of eternity. The abnormal has become the "new normal," and many hardly notice what is really going on.

The apostle Paul adds, "But you, brethren, are not in darkness, so that this Day should overtake you as a thief. You are all sons of the light and sons of the day. We are not of the night nor of darkness. Therefore let us not sleep as others do, but let us watch and be sober" (1 Thessalonians 5:4–6).

The Bible provides divine insight into what is coming upon this world. The prophecies of Daniel and Revelation combined give us inside information. They reveal the amazing events that will soon break upon this world. The Bible's final book, Revelation, unmasks the plans of Satan and reveals the plans of God for an end-time generation. Revelation 18 especially focuses on the major events leading up to the climax of human history. This passage describes what is coming in rather specific details.

The apostle John states:

"After these things I saw another angel coming down from heaven, having great authority, and the earth was illuminated with his glory" (Revelation 18:1).

The angel descends from the glorious presence of God in

the throne room of the universe and is commissioned to proclaim God's last message to warn the inhabitants of the earth with what is coming.

The text says that the angel comes with "great authority." The New Testament Greek word for authority is *exousia*. Jesus uses this word in the Gospel of Matthew in harmony with the sending out of His disciples. In Matthew 10:1 Jesus gives His disciples "authority" over the principalities and powers of hell. He sends them out with the divine power to be victorious in the battle between good and evil. In Matthew 28 He once again sends them out, but this time with "all authority . . . in heaven and on earth" to "go therefore and make disciples of all the nations" (verses 18, 19).

Going forth with the authority of the living Christ, who in His life and death triumphed over the principalities and powers of hell, the New Testament church lightened the earth with the glory of God. In a few short years the disciples proclaimed the gospel to the then-known world (Colossians 1:23). At the end time the Holy Spirit will be poured out in unprecedented power. The gospel will rapidly be spread to the ends of the earth. Thousands will be converted in a day. God's grace and truth will impact the entire planet.

The devil is not going to surrender without a major fight. We will soon enter the battle of the ages between good and evil. Paul's counsel to the Ephesians speaks to us with increasing relevance today. "Finally, my brethren, be strong in the Lord and in the power of His might. Put on the whole armor of God, that you may be able to stand against the wiles of the devil. For we do not wrestle against flesh and blood, but against principalities, against powers, against the rulers of the darkness of this age, against spiritual hosts of wickedness in the heavenly places" (Ephesians 6:10–12).

Notice carefully the clarity of Paul's statement and his counsel. We are in a battle between good and evil. This is no make-believe, fictitious struggle. It is real. Thus Paul's counsel: "Be strong in the Lord and in the power of His might."

The Victorious Christ

In this battle Jesus is our power in weakness. Jesus is our strength in trial. Jesus is our light in darkness. Jesus is our victory in temptation. Jesus is our hope in despair. Jesus is our wisdom in our confusion. Jesus is our healer in sickness. Jesus is our mighty conqueror in the fierce battle between good and evil as we stand in the power of His might.

We saw this battle played out before our eyes recently in Africa. Our meetings were held in Mwanza, Tanzania. Tens of thousands of people attended. Many of them had a strong belief in witchcraft, the power of charms, the influence of their dead loved ones, and the magical power of the witch's spells and demonic forces. We personally experienced the power of God in miraculous deliverances from the grip of demonic forces. Here are just two experiences to illustrate this point. Witches often use charms to place a curse on people. A curse cannot be placed on a child of God. Jesus plainly said, "And I give them eternal life, and they shall never perish; neither shall anyone snatch them out of My hand" (John 10:28). These curses impact only those who believe in them and whose faith is not anchored completely in Jesus.

One of the village witches placed a curse on her devil charms and placed these charms on a narrow village pathway.

The curse she placed on these charms was such that whoever stepped on them would immediately experience excruciating pain in their feet and legs. A poor village woman walked down the path and stepped on these charms. Immediately she experienced horrible leg and foot pain. She suffered for 10 long years. She sought help from witch doctors who she felt were stronger than the one who had placed the curse upon her. She searched and searched, but no one could help her. She visited Christian churches, but found no power for relief there, either. Finally, in the providence of God she met some committed Bible-believing Adventist Christians. They began studying the Bible with her. Sensing her desperate plight, they gave her money for the long, arduous bus journey to our meetings in Mwanza. We established a prayer tent, where approximately 1,000 prayer warriors prayed earnestly for people throughout the day. Deliverances from the powerful forces of evil took place in that tent on a daily basis.

As our Adventist prayer warriors sought God in her behalf and laid hands upon this village woman with her legs in such pain, the power of the Holy Spirit came upon her. She was immediately healed. Her pain was gone. She left rejoicing in the Lord, attended our meetings, and made her decision to be baptized in full surrender to Jesus Christ. The power of God is greater than the power of the evil one. There is no power on earth that Jesus has not already overcome. He is the mighty conqueror.

My colleague Geoffrey Mbwana is a Tanzanian. One evening as we gathered to pray and share experiences after our evangelistic meeting in the stadium, Pastor Mbwana encouraged us to pray for a woman tormented by demons. In fact, she claimed the demons had slashed her with a machete. As Pastor Mbwana met with her he witnessed the terrible cuts all over her body, some of which were bloody and fresh. Since the demonic attacks, this woman was so traumatized she was unable to speak and had to make signs with her hands.

In absolute desperation and horror the girl's mother brought her to our meetings. Pastor Mbwana visited with this tormented woman on a number of occasions. He saw her open wounds and believed her story to be true. She was brought to the prayer tent. Earnest prayer was offered, a terrible struggle ensued, and this girl was miraculously delivered. Pastor Mbwana reported to our staff that he had just come from an interview with her, and she was a changed person. She was calm and peaceful and could now speak.

The apostle Paul reminds us that "the weapons of our warfare are not carnal but mighty in God for pulling down strongholds" (2 Corinthians 10:4).

In Christ the devil is a defeated foe. Whatever attacks that you face, whatever temptations that the evil one throws at you, whatever challenges that you are confronted with, whatever difficulties that you experience, face Satan in the name of Jesus. He has never lost a battle with the devil yet. He is the mighty conqueror pulling down the strongholds of hell, triumphing over the powers of evil, and defeating the enemy in our behalf.

The weapons of our warfare are spiritual, and not earthly or carnal.

There is power in prayer.

There is power in the Word of God.

There is power in the gospel of Christ.

There is power in Jesus to defeat the devil every time.

Every night in Mwanza we received stories of conversions, miraculous deliverances, people set free from Satan's grip, and numerous reports of people being converted and baptized. One of my favorite pictures is of a woman who had been in bondage to evil spirits standing by a pile of ashes at her baptism. When I inquired, "What's that beside her on the ground?" the response was simple: the ashes of all her charms and occult books that she had burned. These newly converted African believers knew that when they were delivered from the clutches of evil by the almighty power of God, they had to get rid of the devil charms.

They could not straddle the fence. It was either Christ or Satan. They kept nothing back. They made an all-out, total, absolute commitment to Christ.

What do you have that should be discarded, abandoned, given up for Christ's sake? The only safety is to listen to the call of Christ and make a clean break. Our only safety is to surrender anything that holds us back from this total commitment to Christ.

Jesus has declared, "If you then being evil, know how to give good gifts to your children, how much more will your heavenly Father give the Holy Spirit to those who ask Him!" (Luke 11:13). The Holy Spirit will come in unlimited power to change our lives and make us witnesses for Christ in this world just before His return.

Is it not wise for us to open our hearts to receive this mighty outpouring of the Spirit?

Is it not wise to ask Jesus to take out of our lives anything that would hinder this mighty outpouring of the Spirit?

Is it not wise to seek God for the heart cleansing necessary to receive the Holy Spirit in all of His fullness?

The Earth Lightened With the Glory of God

Let us notice next Revelation 18:1: "And the earth was illuminated with his glory." Throughout Revelation there are three words that are linked together. They are "glory," "honor," and "power."

We see these words also in Revelation 4:11: "You are worthy, O Lord, to receive glory and honor and power."

Consider Revelation 5:13: "Blessing and honor and glory and power be to Him who sits on the throne, and to the Lamb, forever and ever." Notice once again the association between glory, honor, and power.

We discover this again in Revelation 19:1: "Salvation and glory and honor and power belong to the Lord our God."

And notice Revelation 21:26: "And they shall bring the glory and the honor of the nations to it."

The great controversy between good and evil in the universe is about God's honor, His reputation. It is about His glory—His character—and it is about His power. Is His power really sufficient to deliver His people from the clutches of the evil one? Is His grace really sufficient for us? Satan, a rebel angel, has declared that God is unjust, that He demands worship but gives little in return. The evil one declares that God's law is arbitrary and restricts our freedom and limits our joy.

Jesus' life, death, and resurrection exploded that myth. The One who created us plunged into this snake pit of a world to redeem us. On the cross He answered Satan's charges and demonstrated that God is both loving and just.

Charmed by His love, concerned about His honor, His end-time people reveal His glory—His loving, self-sacrificing character—to a self-centered, godless world, and the earth is illuminated by the character of God.

Remember when Moses asked God to show him His glory? God said, "I will make all My goodness pass before you" (Exodus 33:19). God's goodness is His character.

The earth will be filled with the glory of God when we are so completely overwhelmed with His love, so totally comprehend its depth, and so fully grasp how amazing that grace is that our characters are changed by His redeeming grace.

As the apostle John declares: "Behold what manner of love the Father hath bestowed on us, that we should be called children of God! . . . Beloved, now we are children of God; and it has not yet been revealed what we shall be, but we know that when He is revealed, we shall be like Him, for we shall see Him as He is" (1 John 3:1, 2).

Living out His love in our personal lives reveals His glory, His character, to the world.

A Debt Too Great to Pay

Our obedience is always the response to His love and empowered by His grace. It is this gratitude for all that Christ has done for us that motivates our behavior and leads us to commit the entirety of our lives to Him. There is a wonderful story that illustrates this point marvelously.

Nicholas II was one of the most beneficent czars of Russia. On one occasion he was visiting the Russian troops stationed in a lonely Cossack fortress.

It was a cold blustering night, and the wind howled

mournfully around the ancient fortress and rattled the windows of an office in which a young man sat. Count Ivanovitch gazed with dull eyes at the fire; there was nothing he could do—he was finished.

Ivan was the darling of society, both in Moscow and St. Petersburg: brave, dashing, handsome, he was everybody's favorite. His father had held high military rank and served the czar faithfully until his death. Now exposure and disgrace loomed before Ivan.

For months he had been living far beyond his means, and he was in deep in debt. One poor choice had led to another. He made a bad situation much worse. He began to steal from the regimental funds. He intended to pay it back someday, but never did. Now it was too late. He had taken too much. His debts rose like a mountain before him. Tomorrow the military auditors were coming to the fortress to check on the accounts.

The table behind him was filled with open account books and ledgers. He reviewed the figures until his head ached. He would be court-martialed, dismissed from his esteemed position, and perhaps imprisoned. Yes, his career was finished.

Gazing moodily into the fire, the guilt-ridden young man cried out, "That is the only way out." He got up and found his pistol and was bringing it back to the fire when the open ledgers and books on the table seemed to draw him. He sat down, went over them again and again, then made some rough calculations on a sheet of paper; it was no good, so, pistol in hand, he went back to his seat by the fire.

There was no hurry; he had about five or six hours left. He stared into the fire and thought he saw in the burnt-out coals a picture of his wasted life. Gazing into the flames, exhausted, discouraged, he dozed off into a deep sleep, still clutching his pistol in hand.

At midnight the czar arrived at the fortress. Coming along the corridor, he was surprised to see a light under the door of the young man's office at that hour. He opened it softly and looked in. A litter of books and ledgers open on the table and his friend, Count Ivanovitch, asleep in a chair with a pistol in his hand—is was what he saw.

Amazed, he went nearer to examine the books, and on the table he found a sheet of paper with the words "What I owe"; a long, long list of figures followed, and at the end a boyish scrawl: "So great a debt; who can pay it?"

The czar looked more closely at his sleeping friend and marked the misery and despair on his face; then he took up a pen, added a few words at the bottom of the page, quietly removed the pistol, and left. As dawn broke, Count Ivanovitch awoke. The day that was to bring the dreaded scrutiny had begun. There was just one way out; but where was the pistol? He got up to search for it; then he went over to the table. It was not there; but he saw something at which he stared incredulously. It was just a sheet of paper covered with a long list of debts in his own writing, but something had been added since he had fallen asleep. Under his last despairing question "Who can pay [so great a debt]?" was now written: "I will. Nicholas, czar."

Strange things happened at the fortress that day. Royal dignitaries came. The auditors arrived. Couriers came and went, and surprisingly, headquarters postponed the military audit for three months. Count Ivanovitch was recalled to the capital for a period of duty at the palace. The czar called him in for an interview, and it was the turning point in his life. He deserved imprisonment but received grace. The compassion, forgiveness, and loving-kindness of the czar led this young man to become straightforward, honorable, and prosperous.

You and I owe a debt that is too great to pay. Our indebtedness is so great that it is far beyond our ability to pay the mountain of debt we owe. The law demands absolute perfect righteousness. Nothing else will do. Jesus was absolutely, perfectly righteous, and He offers us His righteousness in place of our sinfulness. The debt we owe is far greater than our capacity to pay, but He paid it all.

As the old hymn says:

"Come, Thou Fount of every blessing,
Tune my heart to sing Thy grace;
Streams of mercy, never ceasing, call for songs of loudest
    praise. . . .

"Oh, to grace how great a debtor
Daily I'm constrained to be!
Let Thy goodness, like a fetter,
Bind me closer still to Thee."

The last message to be proclaimed to a world engulfed in spiritual darkness carried by three angels in the midst of heaven is "Fear God and give glory to Him" (Revelation 14:7). There is no glory in our works, no glory in our righteousness, no glory in our goodness. All glory goes to God.

This is the opposite of the false teaching of the religious

confusion of so many churches. A faith based on human works or rooted in human opinion rather than the Word of God will not stand in earth's last great crisis. Our text proclaims, "And he cried mightily with a loud voice, saying, 'Babylon the great is fallen, is fallen, and has become a dwelling place of demons. . . . For all the nations have drunk of the wine of the wrath of her fornication, the kings of the earth have committed fornication with her, and the merchants of the earth have become rich through the abundance of her luxury' " (Revelation 18:2, 3).

Demonic forces control spiritual Babylon. All nations have drunk the wine of her fornication. Wine represents false doctrine. People become confused in their thinking and mistake error for truth and conclude that truth is error. They turn from the plain truths of God's Word to human opinions and tradition.

Fornication is an illicit union. Notice carefully who unites in this end-time confederacy. There is spiritual Babylon, or false religion based on human teachings.

You might recall that the origin of Babylon is the Tower of Babel, so let's briefly review Genesis 11 and gain some amazing insights about the symbolism of Babylon. Notice Genesis 11:4: "And they said, 'Come, let us build ourselves a city, and a tower whose top is in the heavens; let us make a name for ourselves.' "

The emphasis on the pronoun "ourselves" suggests that they insist that they are on their own. Building the tower is a way of establishing their independence from God. The builders of Babel intend to create a secular civilization separate from God.

The Hebrew word for tower is *migdal.* It is related to the word *gadal,* which means great. It implies the idea of ambition and glory. The purpose of the builders is obviously a spiritual ambition to replace God. They push themselves upward because they refuse to believe in the God who comes down. They want to go up to heaven by their works, but Jesus came down from heaven to accomplish for us what we could never accomplish for ourselves.

This very word *gadal,* which is associated with the Tower of Babel and spiritual Babylon, is also used to describe the little horn or antichrist power of Daniel 7. The little horn, or antichrist, also attempts to exalt itself to the heavens, placing his authority above the authority of God, casting down the truth of God and changing God's law.

Babylon unites with the "kings of the earth" and the "merchants of the earth." Revelation 18 pictures a union of apostate or false religions, political powers—the nations of the earth, and the financial institutions or economic powers. This threefold union unites in a confederacy of evil to eventually persecute the people of God.

Revelation 18 is God's final appeal to all humanity. "And I heard another voice from heaven saying, 'Come out of her, my people, lest you share in her sins, and lest you receive of her plagues' " (verse 4).

Where are most of God's people? In Babylon. And what is God's final call? "Come out of her, my people, lest you share in her sins." What is sin? It is "the transgression of [God's] law" (1 John 3:4, KJV). God is calling His people to come out of every lawbreaking church. Why is God making this final call now? Revelation 18:5 tells us: "For her sins have reached to heaven, and God has remembered her iniquities."

There comes a point when God says, "Enough."

In the days of Noah, God said, "Enough."

In the days of Sodom and Gomorrah, God said, "Enough."

In the days of Babylon, God said, "Enough."

In the last days of earth's history, God will say, "Enough."

Her sins have reached to heaven, and God has remembered her iniquities.

Where are we in the stream of time? Where are we in the panorama of last-day events? We are poised on the verge of a religious, political, and economic union.

The accumulated figures of sin are rapidly reaching their limit in God's record book.

God is preparing a people to proclaim the marvels of His grace, the greatness of His love, the goodness of His character, the righteousness of His law, and the beauty of His truth. God is on the move. He is getting ready to do a mighty thing through His people. "This gospel of the kingdom will be preached in all the world as a witness to all the nations, and then the end will come" (Matthew 24:14).

The nations of earth will hear God's final message to humanity. Every person will have an opportunity to hear and respond to God's invitation to be saved in His kingdom.

God will have a group of people who have bathed in His righteousness and are justified by His grace and sanctified through His power.

They love His truth, live His truth, and proclaim His truth. They count all things but loss for Christ. He is their all in all. They care not for earthly fame or human accolades. Position, prestige, and earthly praise mean little to them. With the apostle Paul they say, "For me, to live is Christ" (Philippians 1:21). Christ is their all in all. Empowered by His Spirit, they proclaim His love and share His grace. The earth is lightened with the glory, the character, of God. The Holy Spirit is poured out in the fullness of His power. Hearts are touched. Lives are changed. The world is reached, and Jesus comes again.

In the fading light of human history, in these critical times in this crisis hour, would you like to say, "Jesus, take away all my human pride; help me to trust in You and You alone, make me what You want me to be, and keep me faithful until You come again"? If that is your prayer, why not spend a quiet moment opening your heart to Jesus and committing your life fully to Him? If you are already a committed Christian, He invites you to take another step in your Christian experience and make a fuller surrender to Him right now. Why not dedicate your life to Him anew right now? You can be part of a mighty movement of God in these climactic hours of earth's history. Will you surrender your life fully to Him right now?

FREE Lessons at www.BibleStudies.com

Call:
1-888-456-7933

Write:
Discover
P.O. Box 999
Loveland, CO 80539-0999

It's easy to learn more about the Bible!